— JAMIE THOM —

A QUIET EDUCATION

CHALLENGING THE EXTROVERT IDEAL IN OUR SCHOOLS

REVIEWS

A Quiet Education is an intelligent, thoughtful and timely contribution to the literature. In his typically informed and disarming style, Jamie questions many established orthodoxies, including those associated with personality and appearance, taking us beneath the surface of teachers and school leaders and asking us to consider our school environments and cultures through a different lens. As our school system struggles to attract and retain a diverse workforce, there are many lessons we can learn through the debates this book provokes. A fascinating read that champions the often-unheard voice of the quiet.

Tom Rees, author and executive director of school leadership at Ambition Institute

I loved reading *A Quiet Education* – its refreshing line of thinking about the thoughts, feelings and experiences of students and teachers in classrooms that are often all too frenetic and loud; where introverted, quieter people are not fully able to be themselves, with the space and time to think, to empathise, to be creative. Supported by a series of excellent "quiet reflections" from a range of contributors and the neatly captured "introspections" that conclude each chapter, Jamie has embarked on a wide-ranging exploration of the quiet philosophy in multiple aspects of school life. I haven't read a book that's made me think so hard about my own practice for a long time. His reflective style is backed with a wide range of very practical, deliverable strategies that certainly demand careful consideration – or introspection! More than anything, I'm sure that a lot of teachers will find the whole spirit of the book inspiring. It's a superb manifesto for a different kind of education.

Tom Sherrington, author and education consultant

Life as a teacher requires you to bring a certain level of energy and drive to the role. When you consider this alongside the pressures we face every day, Jamie's book is a fascinating and vital reminder that things don't have to be so physically and mentally exhausting. For me, Jamie has an unrivalled ability to make the implicit explicit. An invaluable and enriching read.

Andy Sammons, teacher and author

A Quiet Education outlines ways in which we can be more nuanced in our thinking about the quiet members of our community, whether children or adults. Full of sensitivity, insight and common sense, it is a call for a kinder way to go about our business. *A Quiet Education* is full of insights and ideas that are likely to benefit everyone in our settings.

Mary Myatt, author and education adviser

In our noisy, busy, distraction-filled modern lives, the need for quiet has never been more important. This excellent book shows schools how to embrace quiet for the benefit of teachers, students and society at large. A must-read!

Adrian Bethune, primary teacher and author

In Jamie's thoughtful and considered book, he asks us to question the traditional expectations we hold of leaders, teachers and students in our schools and classrooms. He challenges our accepted notions and asks us to consider the value of quiet virtues in modern schools. Reading Jamie's book made me think about how we need to create environments in schools in which students, teachers and leaders can authentically be themselves.

Kulvarn Atwal, executive headteacher and author

Personality is an interesting and at times controversial area of psychology, with relatively little agreement about the relative roles of nature and nurture (other than that both are important!) and with a multitude of competing theories. One thread that runs consistently through the area, though, from the work of Carl Jung to modern experimental psychology, is the idea of extroversion and introversion – that some people respond better than others to complex social situations.

As a teacher, it is easy to see why this idea would be important to education. Some pupils (and indeed some colleagues) appear to prefer classes to be noisy, busy and fast-moving. Others prefer calm, order and quiet. Are we catering for everyone? On some levels, this is an ethical issue, because approaches to schooling that simply don't suit some individuals are exclusionary. But there is also an argument on the basis of efficacy. Moments of quiet reflection can play a key role in giving a person time to think deeply, to problem-solve and to take time to retrieve information from memory, which is exactly why new teachers are often told to increase "wait time" after asking questions. Moments of thoughtful mind-wandering can boost creativity, too.

This book helps to highlight the problematic nature of some educational trends (for example, group discussions as a default teaching strategy) and it makes a convincing case for the value of building in opportunities for calm, quiet moments throughout the day, for pupils and staff alike.

Jonathan Firth, psychology teacher, teacher educator, author and researcher

A manifesto for tranquil teaching and teaching tranquility. *A Quiet Education* is as soothing as it is informative.

Peps Mccrea, author and dean of learning design at Ambition Institute

First Published 2020

by John Catt Educational Ltd,
15 Riduna Park, Melton,
Woodbridge, Suffolk IP12 1QT
01394 389850
enquiries@johncatt.com
www.johncatt.com

Tel: +44 (0) 1394 389850
Fax: +44 (0) 1394 386893
Email: enquiries@johncatt.com
Website: www.johncatt.com

ISBN: 978 1 912906 75 8

Set and designed by John Catt Educational Limited

CONTENTS

FOREWORD

A classroom, somewhere, circa 1993.

"So, Andrew, can you share your thoughts on this matter?"

I had hoped that by averting my eyes she would not see me, that by looking down at the desk I could shroud myself in some sort of invisibility cloak. But now I was hopelessly exposed and I could feel myself heating up, boiling over – cheeks flushing, hands perspiring, neurons connecting and disconnecting at furious random. The thing was, I knew the answer but I just could not find the words, I just could not say it. The seconds passed by shamefully, the disdain of my classmates almost palpable as 30 pairs of eyes bored their way into my hunched back. And then, release. She gave up – as she always did – and asked Nick instead, who cheerfully gave her the answer she was looking for.

For painfully shy and introverted teenagers, a day at school can feel like a day in the trenches. You are always on guard, often quietly terrified, always alert for the next potential threat. As Jamie Thom observes in this excellent book, the modern school and school system seem to be perfectly designed for the extrovert personality: the noisy corridors, the large groupings, the lack of spaces designated for quiet reflection and thought. I must admit that even though I always enjoyed learning, as an introverted secondary pupil I found school to be an excruciating trial.

I have now been a classroom teacher for 14 years. To some extent I have learned how to cover up my naturally shy disposition, and I have even learned to enjoy the thrill of speaking in front of hundreds of adults. Even now, though, I struggle to think on my feet in meetings and prefer to share my ideas in writing. In my personal life, I value time on my own – my ideal holiday location is always somewhere way out in the sticks as far away from the rest of human civilisation as possible!

It is estimated that introverts make up at least one-third of people. The proportion may be even higher in Britain, where we tend to be a little more taciturn and reserved than our European and transatlantic friends. That means that ten or more students in your class of 30 are likely to find an average school day to be socially exhausting. In light of this, Jamie asks a series of important questions. Do we let the needs of extroverts dominate our thoughts in schools? Do we provide adequate support for our introverted students? And, perhaps most importantly, what are the advantages of quietness in the modern school?

The extrovert-introvert continuum cuts across divisions in parent income, class, ethnicity and gender. Yet it is still a very real and important difference in our schools. Not only does Jamie challenge the unfair way that schools seem to be set up for extrovert children, but he also seeks to celebrate the qualities and benefits of introversion. In a sense, this book acts as a paean to those forgotten children in your class: the silent and the shy, the "beige" and the supposedly "passive" – those children who blossom on the inside not the outside.

The beauty of this book is that it doesn't just cover how to work with quiet students – although it does this, and does this well. But it also provides excellent advice for quiet teachers. Featuring a huge number of case studies written by introverted teachers, the book shows how quiet people make for very effective educators. Louder and successful and extroverted teachers will learn much from the book too. For example, the benefits of speaking softly, the benefits of quiet behaviour management and the benefits of becoming a leader who listens carefully to others.

A Quiet Education is a celebration of the personal world of young minds, classrooms and schools, a gentle antidote to the brash confidence, incessant sound and absurd pace of modern schooling. All of this is narrated in Jamie's soothing, friendly and supportive voice, a voice of much-needed balance and honesty in the cacophonous educational landscape we find ourselves in.

I hope that you enjoy the quiet time you spend with this book as much as I did.

Andy Tharby, author and editor of the
Making Every Lesson Count *book series*

For Christopher.
Life is so much louder, but unimaginably better,
since you arrived in our lives.
Thank you.

A QUIET INTRODUCTION

This above all: to thine own self be true
And it must follow, as the night the day
Thou canst not then be false to any man
William Shakespeare, Hamlet

Schools are anything but quiet. Their walls reverberate with noise, with a hubbub of activity that begins long before the bell loudly dictates the start of the day. The interpersonal demands are huge: talk and communication dominate every space.

For those of us who are more inclined to quiet, it can be an exhausting experience.

To the untrained eye it may not appear obvious, but quiet temperaments are just as present inside the school walls as more gregarious ones. The adjectives that define them are ubiquitous and often anything but celebratory: shy, introverted, reclusive, sensitive, guarded, private, withdrawn and antisocial are just a few.

We often define these students as hardworking *but* quiet. The recipients of that dreaded conjunction are frequently prodded (by parents, by teachers, by their peers) to "come out of their shells". How often are they perceived as inferior, intellectually and professionally, as a result of their quieter traits? How often is being quiet seen as a characteristic to overcome rather than celebrate?

Modern education, and indeed modern life, can offer little encouragement for the solitude of these individuals. The reality is that in our schools, as microcosms for society as a whole, being extroverted and outgoing is considered normal and therefore desirable. It is a mark of happiness, confidence and leadership. In classrooms, well-intentioned teachers seek frequent discussion and encourage quick, loud vocal input from students. Our young people exist in a 24-hour culture of communication and dialogue in which the message is that speaking up, standing up, will help them to succeed.

Quiet is often actively discouraged in classrooms. And when teachers do demand quiet, its relationship to punishment is made very clear for students through the subsequent enforced silence. If the adjective "quiet" is used, it is often pejorative: "Daniel is a lovely student, but he is very quiet. He really needs to speak up more."

In this book, I will consider the psychological impact of this flippant dismissal of quiet. I will address what I feel are important questions: how can we encourage greater acceptance and celebration of quiet virtues in modern schools? How can we promote the importance of quiet virtues in building both character and learning?

This book serves as an unashamed cheerleader for all that is quiet, challenging the notion that collaboration and noise should be at the heart of what happens in schools.

I will examine the ways in which we can help quieter students to navigate this extroverted world and achieve their potential. And I will argue that the need to educate and guide our students on the value of quiet is more relevant and important now than ever.

Schools may be dominated by louder, more loquacious and more confident students, but in each classroom there are young people who may not rush to volunteer answers, who may be more hesitant and more reserved. These are the students who pass through the day without contributing verbally, quietly persevering. They, and the following questions, will be our focus in **Part I: Quiet for students**.

- Why should teachers be more aware of the differences between extroversion and introversion?

- How can we ensure that quieter students feel comfortable and confident in lessons?

- What can we do to improve the nature of classroom dialogue?

- Is there a place for group work in classrooms?

- How can we maximise the potential of silence in lessons?

- How can we build more effective relationships with quieter students?

- How can we help them to share their rich inner worlds?

Quiet is not, of course, limited to students. The reality is that many teachers are not naturally outgoing. Some have to channel huge amounts of energy in order to present the extroverted persona that teaching demands. They may find themselves overwhelmed at the end of the day, their energy sapped by the constant interaction that a day in school requires.

These individuals may run for cover when social events are called. In meetings and staff training, their vocal contributions may not match the level of passion and reflection they have for their profession. In fact, they may present as completely anonymous. The instruction "now get into groups and discuss" can horrify them. They might be troubled by impostor syndrome and plagued with doubts about their capacity to teach effectively. It is this self-doubt that fills them with empathy for their students and often makes them wonderful teachers.

There is no magic bullet for the perfect teacher persona and authenticity is vital to success in the classroom. But, as we will discover in this book, there is much to gain from embracing quiet virtues in our teaching and even in our leadership. Quiet leadership in schools is not, despite what some might like to loudly claim, an oxymoron. In these pages we will discover ways in which quiet leadership can thrive in schools. We will consider how quiet leaders can build meaningful relationships, and an understanding of their colleagues, in order to have a significant impact on the lives of young people.

For those of us who lack the confidence to enter roles that require a more extrovert presence, we will examine how we can take the steps without overwhelming our dispositions. Examining our motivation for working in education will be part of this process. Even Doug Lemov, the leadership guru who wrote *Teach Like a Champion*, has said, "I'm a huge introvert. It's strange to me that I do what I do, and like it as much as I do."

In **Part II: Quiet for teachers and leaders**, the following questions will be the focus:

- What can we learn from quiet teachers and leaders?

- How can we find ways to ensure that their strengths are disseminated and their qualities recognised?

- What do they do in their classrooms that we can all learn from?

- What might be the impact of a quieter behaviour management strategy?

- What can prevent burnout among teachers?

- If all teachers embraced a quieter approach to the school day, what might the result be?

- What can we learn from quieter teacher improvement strategies in coaching, reflection and reading?

The learning that takes place in classrooms, where personality dynamic plays such an important role, is often underpinned by invisible and quiet skills. Solitude is a vital precursor for expert performance and for finding what the psychologist Mihaly Csikszentmihalyi calls "flow" – the conditions in which we find ourselves immersed in a task. Classrooms in which extroversion dominates, which are noisy and intense, could in fact be limiting young people's ability to think clearly and to harness the inner dialogue that is so vital to their learning.

The reality is that any final output from our young people is produced in quiet: it is the product of their own understanding and knowledge. Just take a moment to picture the eerie and intimidating silence of an examination hall. While this is clearly not the only purpose of our teaching, are we really doing enough to equip our students with the skills to succeed in these conditions? Are we helping them to enter the world with the ability to think and act autonomously?

Quiet is a source of huge potential in developing lifelong skills that transcend the classroom. In **Part III: Quiet and introspective skills**, the following questions will be our focus:

- What is the secret to improved concentration, motivation and discipline for students?

- What can improve the individual practice we ask students to complete?

- How can we help them to monitor their own thinking?

- How can we improve their ability to meaningfully reflect on their learning?

- What can we do to improve their self-esteem, creativity and motivation?

- How can we cultivate the quiet qualities of listening and empathy?

I have a personal mission in writing this book. I freely admit that I embody every introverted and quiet cliché. I am happier at home reading or writing than I am out socialising, I border on invisible in staff meetings, and I find myself severely lacking in conversation after a day in school. This cocktail makes me scintillating company and can often lead to conflict with my remarkably extroverted wife! It doesn't, however, detract from what I know is a very energetic and enthusiastic classroom presence. My students are often surprised when I refer to myself as a quiet and more introverted individual. This is an exploration for later in the book – are our personas more fluid than we think?

Quiet qualities prevail in my family. Deep in the beautiful Highlands of Scotland, surrounded by fields and inquisitive cows (and books), my mother and father live a quiet life in nature. Both encapsulate all quiet clichés, but (there is that pesky conjunction again) have devoted their lives to young people and education. My mother was a nurturing and life-changing primary school teacher for 25 years. My father continues to enthuse and inspire young people after 35 years of teaching English in the same school. I should know: he taught me and was very much an inspiration for my becoming an English teacher.

One of the aims of this book is to give voice to quiet teachers like my parents; to allow them to articulate what they do every day in the classroom with humility, patience and love. As we shall see, this collaborative drive is at the heart of what will make us stronger as a profession. Each chapter concludes by giving voice to one of these practitioners, as they seek to understand what they are doing and achieving in education. Through these "quiet reflections", we will see just how important it is that schools and classrooms are representative of all personalities and characteristics.

This book was not written to add additional work to teachers' already busy lives. Nor does it ask us to revolutionise our practice. Instead it is about subtle adjustments, interpersonal awareness and an increased recognition of the ways in which we can build effective relationships with all our students.

I hope to begin a dialogue that is led by a loud declaration: a quiet education will lead us to a greater understanding of our students, ourselves, our capacity for leadership and, vitally, how young people learn best.

PART I
QUIET FOR STUDENTS

People are so complicated. It's like every new person is a completely new roll of the dice
Marilynne Robinson, The Givenness of Things

CHAPTER 1
THE INTROVERT-EXTROVERT
CONTINUUM

It is Iona's first day of primary school. She is an intuitive, quiet and sensitive child who enters the classroom tentatively. Gazing around, she sees groups of students engaged in excited chatter. She takes a deep breath and walks forward...

We are all complex individuals. Our dispositions are formed by a unique blend of environment, upbringing and inherent qualities. They are also more fluid than we might think: we could be the consummate extrovert in some circumstances and behave with real reticence in others.

Like many people with a quieter and shyer disposition (not that the two always go hand in hand), I have spent many of my 33 years on some kind of self-improvement mission. The reality, however, is that there is no magic button we can press to change our personalities (and we shouldn't really need to). The self-help section of the bookshop and I know each other well, yet our relationship has never blossomed into meaningful outcomes. There is still lingering bitterness about that £10 I invested in *Confidence*, and about the distinct lack of oratory transformation stemming from *Transform your Public Speaking*.

The experience of Oliver Sacks, the writer and neurologist, would imply that my labours are not likely to lead to the confidence metamorphosis that I have often yearned for. Sacks wrote this in his final book, *Gratitude*, shortly before he died at the age of 82: "I am sorry I have wasted (and still waste) so much time; I am sorry to be as agonizingly shy at eighty as I was at twenty; I am sorry that I speak no languages but my mother tongue and that I have not traveled or experienced other cultures as widely as I should have done."

Yet Sacks, as we all have to, found a way to navigate the world and leave behind a remarkable output and impact. The following words, also from *Gratitude*, are particularly inspiring: "My predominant feeling is one of gratitude. I have loved and been loved; I have been given much and I have given something in return; I have read and travelled and thought and written ... Above all I have been a sentient being, a thinking animal, on this beautiful planet, and that in itself has been an enormous privilege and adventure."

Emotional comfort

From an educator's perspective, personality and teaching are deeply interconnected. Our lives, after all, would be magnificently dull if we were always faced with 30 versions of the same individual. One of the reasons we enter the profession is an enjoyment of and respect for the dizzying diversity of character among young people. Our purpose is not to try to engineer or change these personalities; rather it is to provide them with the conditions in which to feel confident to learn and develop.

Teachers can strive to help young people see the value in their own temperaments. Yet, from my conversations with young people and parents in preparation for this book, it appears that this sensitive encouragement and nurturing is not as present in schools as we would hope.

An example that illustrates this profoundly came from the mother of a girl who had just started secondary school. At the end of Year 6, the child's teacher had written in her report: "She is a shy, unassuming and quiet girl." The headteacher's final comment, however, was much more empowering: "You don't have to be an extrovert in life to achieve well, and I encourage you to keep working as hard as you are and just be you. Well done."

I asked the child's mother, the science teacher Dr Emma Angell (@emmalangell), how her daughter had found the transition to secondary school:

> "She is quieter and more reflective. She thinks before she speaks. She's shy around strangers and has always found starting a new academic year difficult.
>
> There would be tears and declarations that last year was better than this year, last year's teacher was nicer than this year's teacher. There would be repeated conversations at parents' evenings about how she should try to contribute more voluntarily: she answered questions when asked but appeared reluctant to put herself forward. Her introverted nature would be described to us as if it were the first time we'd been told, or as if we hadn't realised that's how she was. Some teachers were more understanding than others, but the overriding impression we got is that extroversion is more valued than introversion.
>
> We would heavily edit the feedback we passed on to our daughter. She has had found transition to secondary very hard, mostly because she's now exposed to more poor behaviour, bad language, sexualised language, and negative attitudes to learning, which she finds most perplexing."

This gives us an insight into the complexity behind any young person's quiet disposition. It lays bare the importance of the core qualities of all effective teachers: empathy and compassion. For students such as these to thrive – for all students to thrive, in fact – they need to feel emotionally comfortable.

Learning and emotion are completely interlinked: a child cannot be motivated or actively present unless they feel secure and understood as a learner. Equally, as teachers we cannot possibly become competent in the classroom, never mind experts, unless we have the capacity to connect and form relationships.

The personality continuum

What is it that influences our temperaments and personalities? The extent to which we might define ourselves as quieter or louder is clearly significant. "Our tendency to be extroverted or introverted is as profound a part of our identities as our gender," writes Susan Cain in her book *Quiet: The Power of Introverts in a World That Can't Stop Talking*. "But there's a subtle bias against introverts, and it's generating a waste of talent and energy and happiness."

This "subtle bias" is enacted unintentionally in classrooms every day. Our quieter students' experience of school can, as we shall see, be heavily influenced by how empathetic and considerate their teachers are. Indeed, lessons are often completely derailed by breakdowns in communication, moments in which compassion and understanding are lost.

To delve into the murky world of nature and nurture, and its influence on our temperament, would detract from the educational focus of this book, so in this chapter we will look only at the personality continuum. For decades, psychologists have used the extrovert-ambivert-introvert continuum as a way to understand our motivations and different ways of looking at the world.

Carl Jung

In many ways the father of the introvert-extrovert theory, Carl Jung first popularised the terms "extraversion" and "introversion" in 1921. According to Jung, the human mind has certain innate characteristics that are "imprinted" on it as a result of evolution. An attitude, according to Jung, is a person's predisposition to behave in a particular way. There are two opposing attitudes: introversion and extraversion/extroversion. He stated: "Each person seems to be energized more by either the external world (extraversion) or the internal world (introversion)."

Jung also acknowledged that nobody is a complete embodiment of one attitude over another: "There is no such thing as a pure extrovert or a pure introvert. Such a man would be in the lunatic asylum."

Myers-Briggs Type Indicator

Jung's work was built upon by Isabel Briggs Myers (1897–1980) and her mother, Katharine Cook Briggs (1875–1968), who wanted to simplify the dense messages and did so by developing the Myers-Briggs Type Indicator. This has become a staple feature of corporate training sessions, usually arriving in the form of a questionnaire. The questions relate to your decision-making processes, your lifestyle and the way you process information. Your personality is then assigned to one of 16 categories.

I have spoken to many teachers who have found Myers-Briggs to be hugely influential on their practice. My mother said the following of her own experience of it: "As part of my CPD, our whole staff in 2006 had a very in-depth training day on Myers-Briggs – a much more detailed questionnaire than those that are online and wonderful follow-up reading to help us make sense of ourselves in the workplace. It enhanced my relationship with my colleagues and headteacher, who was the only other INFJ [personality type]. We understood each other better and the impact our introversion or extroversion had on our practice as teachers, but also our contribution to meetings and the life of the school. It was one of the most useful training days I ever had. It also helped me notice the differing types of personalities in the classroom far more easily."

I completed a few online versions of the Myers-Briggs questionnaire and it seems I take after my mother:

INFJ

Introvert (97%) – Intuitive (3%) – Feeling (16%) – Judging (19%)

- You have strong preference of Introversion over Extraversion (97%)
- You have marginal or no preference of Intuition over Sensing (3%)
- You have slight preference of Feeling over Thinking (16%)
- You have slight preference of Judging over Perceiving (19%)

Apparently I am among just 1% of the population, with the rarest of all personality types – I feel this merits some kind of display badge. Isabel Briggs Myers can tell me more about this exciting discovery: "The visions of the INFJs tend to concern human welfare, and their contributions are likely to be made independent of a mass movement." Sounds about right: I have had a few quizzical looks about my early-morning penning of a book examining the role of quiet in education!

Is reflecting on our own temperaments self-indulgent, or might it help us to function better both professionally and personally? I would go with the latter: self-awareness is a vital part of effective teaching. Knowing ourselves and our motivations can help us to navigate the interpersonally demanding world of teaching in a modern school.

Extroverted students

Essentially, extroversion means being outward-facing. Extroverted students are those who consume more of our energy in the classroom, in positive and negative ways. In social situations they are likely to be the dominant member, and they take pleasure and reward in high-stimulation activities. They often have a breadth of interests and throw themselves into challenges.

My wife is the embodiment of an extrovert: she is always keen to socialise and attend parties, and she builds a wide range of friendships easily. Jung theorised that extroverts are likely to be happier and more optimistic, which is a fair reflection of my Morrissey-style pessimism and indeed our marriage!

In the classroom, extroverted students take much more of a lead; they are keen to offer answers or challenge those around them. They prefer to talk through learning and problems, so dive head first into activities and topics without pausing to reflect and perhaps gain greater understanding. They crave communication and group work, are keen to teach others and might find solitary work more difficult.

Introverted students

The word "introversion" first appeared in 1654, in correlation with "introspection". It stems from the modern Latin *introvertere: intro-* (to the inside) and *vertere* (to turn). It suggests satisfaction found in a rich inner world – in contemplation, in reflection and in time spent alone.

Introversion is often mistakenly correlated with shyness: some introverts may indeed be shy, but certainly not all. The word "shy" implies being frightened or intimidated in social settings, but introverts are often just more energised by their own company. In fact, they can be hugely skilled in social situations, and as powerful observers they can be effective, empathetic listeners.

Such students can appear aloof and more complex. They may be fizzing with ideas and activity, but they are less inclined to share that with others. Their brains process information in a different way to their more extroverted peers, and they may appear to be slightly unfocused or even dreamy. They may be onlookers in group tasks or specifically ask to be assigned roles such as timekeeper or scribe. They are often most at ease when working on sustained individual tasks, and may appear to be disciplined and conscientious. They may prefer paired activities with a trusted partner.

It is interesting to consider Albert Einstein's experience of school. In the biography *Einstein: A Life*, Denis Brian writes that Einstein was seen as "quiet and withdrawn – the onlooker" and was perceived to be "dull-witted". In his career, however, Einstein talked frequently about the importance he placed on being alone and allowing time for reflection, going as far as to say: "Be a loner. That gives you time to wonder, to search for the truth. Have holy curiosity. Make your life worth living." Einstein's own relative anonymity in the school environment is a reminder of the unique depths that our students may be hiding from us.

Human complexity

Human nature is hugely complex and cannot, of course, be reduced to a checklist (or indeed a questionnaire). Labelling our students as entirely introverted or extroverted may influence how they view themselves and their behaviours, but imposing such limitations on them is certainly not what we want to do. What we should, and can, do is normalise the varying personality types and seek to celebrate their qualities.

Now we have an understanding of why some students may present as quiet, we can start to unpick the ways in which we can help these students to thrive in the classroom. Our teaching will always need to balance the needs of all students, and to suggest that it be completely re-engineered towards our more introverted students would be wrong.

The reality is that the best teachers are those who can motivate all students, extrovert or introvert, to achieve their best. The ability to connect with quieter students is of vital importance if, as research has hinted, they comprise a third or more of the young people in our classrooms. It should be a key focus of our pedagogical skills, just as we are armed with ways to stretch and challenge our students, or provide support for those who might be finding the work more demanding.

This starts with emotional security, with providing an environment that tells young people that regardless of how loud they are, or how often they contribute in lessons, they matter. It begins at a point of real significance: the importance of names. We will explore this in chapter 2…

A quiet reflection

This reflection is written by the mother of a young person. She asked to remain anonymous.

After her first day in a new nursery, my four-year-old daughter came home and told me that she had not been able to talk to anyone and that she had "felt invisible".

Jump forward eight years.

"You don't say much, do you? I can't really do this interview if you don't talk."

Those words were said in her second year of secondary school, in a one-to-one pastoral meeting with the adult who was meant to be her go-to person. My daughter had struggled through her first year, feeling like a fish out of water, clinging to one good friend in an environment where she felt she didn't fit because she liked studying and didn't care about three-stripe trainers or being popular.

She was studious and very able, but no one really realised that, or encouraged her, in her early years at secondary school. I could see that she was unhappy but felt powerless to do much, other than encourage her at home and try to get her teachers to see through her introversion.

Her school reports were full of the same: she was doing well but needed to speak out more. In fact, several implied that she needed to put more effort into her work, equating putting a hand up to answer in class with effort. At home, she would tell me of the absolutely paralysing fear that she felt at the thought of being asked something in class, or putting her hand up.

In some ways, her inability to speak out frustrated me, because I could see that it was stopping her teachers realising how capable she was. I remember trying to work on it with her at home and encouraging her to push herself to be more conversational. Otherwise, I warned her, she might gain a reputation of being rude or aloof. Imagine my horror when I finally read an article on the dos and don'ts of parenting introverted children and it had this "encouragement" firmly in the "don't" column.

As a drama teacher, I have always been committed to helping children develop all their expressive capabilities; I viewed the spoken voice as just one tool in our expressive armoury. But witnessing my daughter's experience in secondary school has made me realise that too many teachers value extrovert tendencies in learners far more than is helpful.

Whoever decided that verbal contributions are more valid than other forms of expression? Whoever ruled that speaking out in front of 30 of your peers is a generically useful skill? Whoever decreed that working in a group is intrinsically more valuable than solitary working?

Now, in her fifth year of secondary school, my girl has a small but solid group of friends who love her for what she is. She has excelled academically, in spite of many of her teachers' attitudes. She is hoping to apply to a top university in a year's time. We are slightly worried that she may not come across well in interview and are trying to rehearse for that scenario. But we are also telling her that she is more than enough just as she is, even if she finds situations like interviews difficult.

My wish would be that schools and teachers could give the same message to all children: you are more than enough. We see you and we hear you.

Introspection

1. How aware are you of the personality continuum in your classroom?

2. Do you approach your interactions with extroverted and introverted students differently?

3. How would you rate yourself on the introvert-extrovert scale? What does your Myers-Briggs rating tell you?

4. How does your rating impact you as a teacher?

5. Are you self-aware – conscious of your own strengths and weaknesses?

6. How well do you know your students as individuals?

CHAPTER 2
QUIET RELATIONSHIPS

David is walking into his third appointment of parents' evening. It is his Spanish teacher. As he enters the room, he sees a flash of panic in Miss Memorando's eyes and a rummaging of papers. There is a pause. "Ah yes, let me see...David."

David sighs (the irony of David being the least challenging name to remember is not lost on him). He waits for some generic comments and then for the dramatic climax: the obligatory "he is hard-working and doing well, but he is very quiet". By the end of the evening, he has heard this phrase nine times.

In discussions about quieter young people, frustration is often expressed. It is common to hear suggestions that they are in some way deficient; that they need to be altered, with other qualities superimposed upon them. In this chapter, rather than seeing quiet students as stuck in some metaphorical prison, we will explore how to accept and value their contributions and nurture their development.

The act of genuine recognition begins very simply: with the use of names. Two years ago, my wife and I had our first child. For months we agonised over a name. Hours of blood, sweat and tears went into the big decision. Our personalities dictated that she spoke at length and deliberated externally, while I pensively reflected in silence. When our delightful wee chap came screaming into the world, my wife decided he didn't "look like" the name she had passionately (and loudly) fought for.

Hazy days of namelessness ensued. Then, in the early hours one morning, my wife uttered a name that hadn't previously crossed either of our minds. Something clicked. We both knew that this would be the name we would be repeating for the rest of our lives.

What's in a name?

Why did we angst over this choice? Well, our names are crucial to our identities: they mark us for all our time on this planet. Maria Konnikova, in an article for *The New Yorker* entitled "Why Your Name Matters", gave them even more significance: "Some recent research suggests that names can influence choice of profession, where we live, whom we marry, the grades we earn, the stocks we invest in, whether we're accepted to a school or are hired for a particular job, and the quality of our work in a group setting. Our names can even determine whether we give money to disaster victims: if we share an initial with the name of a hurricane, according to one study, we are far more likely to donate to relief funds after it hits."

The way we feel when a person we have spent time with forgets our name, or uses it incorrectly, proves the emotional importance of names. We shrink. We feel anonymous. And we are left with the nagging sense that, ultimately, we don't matter.

Invisible students

Sammy was a quiet, unassuming student in my first A-level literature class, almost ten years ago. She rarely contributed verbally, but she brought a conscientiousness and care to her work that I have rarely seen surpassed. Unsurprisingly, she left school with a glittering array of top grades.

When I contacted her and explained the purpose of this book, I asked her what she had found most frustrating about her experience as a quieter student in secondary school. She was very clear: "Feeling invisible – the sense that teachers don't acknowledge you. They gloss over you as they go straight to the kids who dominate the lessons."

She elaborated on this notion of invisibility: "The sense that some teachers don't even know your name."

The parents of quieter children see the impact of this feeling – the feeling that they don't matter – and how the decisions made by schools can lead to further alienation. Maggie Mumford, an English teacher, wrote to me about the experience of her son:

"If you are the parent of a second/third-set child, who is neither sporty nor musical, and whose emotional needs mean they can only cope with the basic school day, you can sometimes feel invisible, particularly to school management, who often use newsletters to celebrate the achievements of the more energetic and conventional students.

Consequently, the introverted or late-developing child can easily go a whole school career without ever being picked for any special events or activities, which, in turn, can make the parent feel alienated from the school. Never featured in any school publications or publicity, they can literally feel invisible. There can be a tendency for schools to use the same set of reliable students, compounding the feeling of inferiority felt by the introverted child and parent. The chosen children are then praised for their commitment and contribution to the school, which can become a self-perpetuating cycle, with certain kids being given confidence-building experiences that have been denied to other, shyer or more introverted students."

The sense that somehow they are not part of the fabric of the classroom, or indeed the school, is not going to help students feel comfortable. We all crave acceptance and community, and being quieter can often mean that you feel left on the periphery or the outside.

Despite our best efforts, there may well be students in our classrooms for whom these words resonate painfully. A significant amount of teachers' attention is absorbed by louder or more challenging students. Often it is forgotten that the majority are no trouble and a large proportion are very quiet – possibly shy, possibly introverted. The first way in which we can signal to them that they matter is by using their name, and using it correctly.

Pronunciation

One stumbling block we may face is how to pronounce those names that appear, intimidatingly, on the register. An anonymous English teacher in the US, known as Shakespeare's Sister, has written about setting a clear intention to know who her students are as individuals:

"At the beginning of every school year, I try to learn all of my 11th graders' names by the end of our first week together. A thing happens every year, though, when I am verifying pronunciations of student names.

This year, it happened with two male students whose names have two possible pronunciations. When I asked them for the correct pronunciation, they both responded, 'Whatever is fine.'

When it happens, as it does every year, I look up from my roster, make eye contact, and say, 'No, it's not. It's your name. Tell me how to say it.'"

This may seem slightly melodramatic, but it is the first step in demonstrating care and respect. Forging a connection and a relationship with an individual begins with learning to pronounce their name.

I spent the first few years of my career teaching in a comprehensive in central London, so wrestling with pronunciation is something I can certainly empathise with. I would always apologise and make light of my poor attempts, resolving to work to conquer names that were unfamiliar to my rather parochial Highland Scottish tongue. I did this to humanise and give humour to the endeavour, revealing to my students that care and respect were at the heart of what happened in my classroom. And there is nothing wrong with highlighting that teachers might feasibly have to recall hundreds of names.

Remembering names

Classrooms should ideally have names reverberating around them at all times, signalling that relationships and people are valued in that space. Deliberately seeking out quieter students and referring to them by name will help them to see you as someone who cares about them. There may be lessons and even days in which their name is not used once, particularly in secondary school.

Schools in which leaders and teachers regularly use names are schools in which you get the sense that individuals matter. When you walk through the corridors and hear students being addressed by name, you recognise that relationships are at the heart of this community. Dr Jill Berry (@jillberry102), the author of *Making the Leap: Moving From Deputy to Head*, shared with me her strategy to ensure that she knows the names of as many students as possible:

> "When I was a headteacher, I decided to teach every Year 7 class for one lesson each week (paired with their 'real' English teacher, so if I had to be out of school, the children were taught anyway). By October half-term I knew all their names, and after doing this for seven years I knew the names of everyone in the senior school.
>
> In retrospect, it was one of the best decisions I made as a head. It's the first step in showing that each individual matters. Those staff who say they can't learn or remember names are the ones who need to work harder to find a strategy that works for them. I used name cards (which the pupils designed themselves), collecting them in at the end of each lesson and handing them out at the start of the next lesson until I didn't need them anymore. (It also helped the pupils learn each other's names.) I found it worked for me to be able to see a face and a name together in one glance. However you do it, do it!"

Memory problems

Although I understand the importance of this name quest, I am one of those teachers who find it more of a struggle. I have a fairly dreadful memory, which is probably why my history career did not blossom beyond the school walls. Writing this book has given me a fresh awareness of my difficulties with remembering names. And my recent relocation from England to Scotland, where I have joined a very diverse comprehensive school in central Edinburgh, has given me a huge number of names to learn.

Here are some methods that have helped me to prevent that moment of panic, in which you gaze into the eyes of one of your students and there is a blank where their name should be.

- **Seating plans**. Before getting to know students as individuals and working out where they will best be placed, a seating plan can be an excellent name-learning mechanism. Most schools now have a way of printing off seating plans that include an image of each student – keeping this with you makes learning names significantly easier. It is also sensible to get every child to say their name when they answer a question for the first week or so.

- **Testing**. Cut out pictures of your students and test yourself. This is, of course, hours of fun, and partners of teachers across the land will know how much this dominates the start of the school year. Pick out five students to begin with and build up to the full class of 30. The effort is worth it in the end, as our students are secretly delighted that we know their names already. Sharing this task with students can be effective: going through the testing process with them is a lighthearted and competitive end to a lesson.

- **Memory cues**. Associate the name of each student with a memory or visual cue. It can help to get them to write or talk about themselves, and alliterative cues can also be handy. Asking students to share particular stories or meanings behind their names can be very useful.

- **Promise to do better**. It is better to use and forget than to not use at all, particularly in the first few weeks of term. Students will understand if you apologise and commit to not making the same mistake again. Repetition is the key here: saying names as many times as possible is the only way I can make sure I'm getting it right.

- **Name checklist**. Putting a tick by a student's name every time you use it can reveal just how much some of them are absorbing your time and attention. There are always those students whose names we learn at the end of the first lesson. Make a conscious effort to get ticks by the names of the quieter individuals who need much more deliberate attention.

- **Workbooks**. A very simple tip is to make sure you hand out the books at the start of the first few lessons. This helps you to remember where students are sitting and their names.

On their level

Body language and style of communication are also important in fostering positive relationships. How often do we talk down to students from a position of authority? This fails to help them feel at ease in our presence and ready to open up about their learning.

Quiet students often require quieter conversations. Physically being on the same level as students and using eye contact can make a significant difference to the quality of interactions. Some teachers appear to be invisible in the classroom. They are always down at their students' level: crouching beside them, sitting alongside them, anything that removes the sense of didactic authority. This serves to relax both them and us, and indicates that we value their thoughts and opinions. It also means that less confident students don't have to project their voices and thus be overheard by others in the room – they are cocooned in a private conversation in which they may comfortable enough to reveal their thinking.

Please and thank you

What else can help our students to feel more accepted and confident? Basic manners are a step in the right direction. Regularly saying "thank you" and "please" helps to establish a culture of care and respect. Teachers need to drive this agenda, modelling it at all times, even when we are trying to defuse a difficult situation.

In classrooms in which basic manners are modelled by teachers, students are much more likely to use them in response, and use them with each other. The expectation of civility can change behaviours and trickle into the lives of students at home.

Positive encouragement

Even praise and positivity can be adapted for more introverted students. I was contacted online by Catrin Ashton (@catrinashton), a teacher from Sheffield, who had just returned from her daughter's rewards evening: "I thought of you at my child's award ceremony today, where many recipients were introduced as, 'He/she is very quiet/introverted *but* has nevertheless achieved blah blah blah.' It made me quite cross."

There is that pesky conjunction again, even when a child's achievements are being rewarded. What message does that send? Our language around quiet can and should be so much more celebratory and positive. Offering praise for the quiet virtues that we will explore later in the book can help: we might comment on excellent listening skills, celebrate a particularly thoughtful piece of writing, or recognise eye contact or moments of empathy that light up a lesson. Praise should not always be reserved for surface-level behaviour – we should also validate deeper, more complex behaviours.

In my mother's primary school classroom, a sign reading "Difference is that wonderful thing we all have in common" was always present. Younger children know this instinctively and are open to valuing others and finding joy in commonality. Arguably, it is only in adolescence and into adulthood that we begin to judge others and set standards of "acceptability". Thus, it is even more important that secondary schools discuss and explore the differences that are present in all classrooms.

Quiet support

Building positive relationships also comes down to recognising when students need help, without them having to explicitly ask for it. One of the members of my old tutor group in the North East of England, now on a gap year before going on to further study, got in touch with his reflections on what it was like to be an introvert in school. They make for interesting reading:

> "Mostly I focused on my own world. It took a while, but in class I learnt to block out everything apart from what I was working on.
>
> I think being quiet in secondary school is a struggle in the first few years, because you don't necessarily have a strong friendship group, so you have to build friendships and that can be hard because you need to be chatty to do that. But eventually you develop a niche for yourself – in my case I was the smart one and developed a reputation that if the teacher was busy, you could come and ask me and I'd know the answer, or have a good shot at it. This was OK as an introvert because it wasn't a prolonged conversation, just a question about work and then they would go away again.
>
> As that develops, you also find a friendship group develops alongside it, of similarly minded individuals with the same interests. After that point it becomes easier because you have a group of people, not necessarily to have to talk with, but to sit with at lunch or in class. It was good to sit with a large group but not have to actively engage all that much.
>
> One of the biggest challenges is learning that it is OK to ask for help, and that you aren't being a nuisance and that the teacher is there to help. Before

you do that, you have a tendency to try and struggle on by yourself, and avoid asking the teacher or anyone around you for help because that's interaction and a nuisance.

The solution for being introverted is not immersion therapy. If someone is quiet and shy, the answer isn't to stand them up at the front of the class. For teachers, it's important that they recognise that someone needs help, and not to make a big deal of it in the middle of class. Instead it is more helpful to ask them quietly afterwards what they need help with, because that reduces the tension in the room for them."

Oliver's thoughtful points suggest the need for real awareness when providing support to students, because they are all different. Some may feel overwhelmed or struggle to access content, but they might not feel comfortable asking for help – we need to think carefully about that need and how we can address it.

We often fall into the trap of asking the ultimately pointless whole-class question "Does everyone understand?", then interpreting silence as reassurance that everyone is clear. Instead, making ourselves available for individual questions, or trying to be available outside of lessons, can give young people opportunities to open up about their difficulties.

Beyond the classroom

One aspect of school that can prove challenging for introverted and quiet students is that although they participate in all subjects, they may secretly have a burning passion for something in particular. How can we discover what interests them – or help them to discover what interests them – and support them on their way?

Microsoft co-founder Bill Gates, a hugely successful introvert, has talked at length about his experience as a quieter student, and about how he was supported to find and channel his passion:

"From a young age, ideally you will have adults in your life, preferably your parents as part of that, some of your teachers, people around you, who like you and they're behind you and they will back you, no matter what goes on, and that gives you enough confidence to go off on a quest and during that quest you try different things out.

If you're lucky when you're very young, you find something you're passionate about. I did when I was 13 years old. I found computers and software. It took me another five years to figure out that was my life's primary work, but that's a lucky thing.

Other people, you know, get up into their 20s or even later before they find what they're passionate about, but proceeding with a certain set of self-confidence, that there are people who care for you, you care for them, that you succeed in their eyes by how you treat them, I think that's pretty basic and it gives you the platform on which to try out new things, to fail, you know. First, you're not going to succeed in various things, so self-confidence is primary and then finding your passion is an adventure, a quest that may take time, and it may switch over the time of your life, but those deep relationships will let you pursue it with vigour."

Nurturing passions

Beyond the classroom, school life is rich in opportunities for young people to find out what motivates them. My recent experience with a group of 20 students has reinforced this. I set up a lunchtime writing club called The Write Lunch, with the aim of publishing a book in memory of a former student at the school. She had been diagnosed with a rare type of cancer at the age of 14 and had died four years later.

Once news spread about the chance to become a published author and raise funds for charity, the popularity of the writing club increased. Although the group was diverse, it did bring together a number of the quieter young people in the school. Some struggled with confidence and were empowered by finding others who shared their passion.

The Write Lunch became a time to pause and escape from the busy school environment. I was amazed by the students' determination to raise money for charity, and by how these more introverted children channelled this drive into more extroverted fundraising tasks. For me, it confirmed that we must find appropriate moments to discover more about our students and to look beyond what they might superficially present in lessons.

This chapter has shown how profoundly important interpersonal relationships are in teaching. For those students who may not demand much attention, a deliberate investment of time is critical. This can be challenging, considering the number of students that we deal with on a daily basis, but recognition, care and time are the building blocks of positive relationships.

In the next chapter, we will consider the complexities of evaluating participation and explore how we use those most ubiquitous of teaching tools: discussion and dialogue.

A quiet reflection

Tom Sherrington (@teacherhead) is the author of a range of education books, including The Learning Rainforest: Great Teaching in Real Classrooms *and* Rosenshine's Principles in Action. *A former headteacher, Tom is now a full-time education consultant. In this post from his blog, teacherhead.com, Tom outlines why using names is so vital.*

When I was in Jakarta at the British International School, the EAL department supported a group of Korean students to stage a protest. They made some placards and, during lesson time, they walked around one of the central areas chanting "Know my name! Know my name!" It was a powerful moment for them – and for me.

It was partly a speaking activity – giving the students an authentic opportunity to have their voices heard – but it was also a genuine chant of protest and frustration. In that context, Korean students were offended by that fact that teachers all too often did not know their names or did not say them correctly. From an English-language background, names like Jung So Min or Kim Hyung Jun can be hard to learn; you don't have reference points around gender or even know the forename-surname protocols. Faced with uncertainty, teachers would often avoid using student names in case they were wrong, or they'd guess and cause offence – making a basic gender error, for example. We discussed this and resolved to do better.

In the UK, the same applies, with teachers needing to engage with students from a range of backgrounds different to their own, where learning names might be more difficult – but actually the "know my name" mantra could apply to any student. It's a pretty basic and reasonable entitlement to expect that our teachers know who we are and can say our names correctly. It seems so obvious but, in reality, it is still something we need to discuss and be explicit about. It matters a great deal to the students – the comforting sense of being known contrasts sharply with the opposite: my teacher doesn't even know my name!

I remember a boy called Mustafa who was always furious if you said MusTAfa; it was definitely MUStafa – and it mattered to him. I feel the same whenever I'm referred to as Tom Sherringham. That's not my name! At KEGS [King Edward VI Grammar School in Chelmsford], there were some long Sri Lankan-origin names that were hard to get right and could trip you up reading out certificates in assembly. Nothing worse than making someone's friends laugh at the moment of trying to celebrate their achievements.

But knowing student names with confidence is also massively empowering to teachers. Once you know your students' names it's so much easier to engage them with questioning: "Syrah…let's hear your idea, what do you think? Joe, Mustafa, what were you saying in your discussion?" I've found that not knowing names is a big inhibitor when it comes to asking questions. And, of course it helps with behaviour management – once you know names, you avoid lumping people together. Instead of "guys" or "everyone" or "back table", you get a much better response if you highlight that it's specifically Stephania and Josef who need to give you their full attention.

As was outlined superbly by Peps Mccrea at the Durrington researchEd event last year [2018], we are not experts in our classrooms until we know our students; we don't know how to teach with optimum effect until we know what they know and how they will respond to feedback of different kinds. Building relationships underpins all good teaching – at an emotional and a technical level. Knowing names is the start of that process.

When I was a head of year, every lunchtime I would go down the lunch queue testing myself on student names early in the term. I took the photos home and studied them, actively trying to learn names and then testing myself in practice the next day. As a teacher, I've always made a seating plan for the sole purpose of learning names, trying to wean myself off referring to it as soon as possible. It's so important. (I've also done the same with staff in any new job. It's horrible for all concerned when, in staff briefing for example, you want to invite someone to give a message but you can't remember their name.)

Whenever I haven't invested time in learning names, I've always felt disempowered – as well as knowing I was giving my students (or staff) a sense of being remote from them. You always get to know the students who excel or who cause lots of problems with behaviour, so it's the middle-ground students where you need to invest time. I would advise that teachers take plenty of time to explore student names, getting pronunciations right, learning surnames as well as first names and discussing uncertainties with the students until you get them right. It's always time well spent.

Introspection

1. Do you use students' names with purpose in your classroom?

2. Who is slipping through your communication channels?

3. What are you doing to make sure you are correctly learning the names of all your students?

4. How do you use body language, positioning and eye contact to communicate with quieter students?

5. Could you make greater use of "please" and "thank you"?

6. Are you aware of students who may need more support but are not confident to ask for it?

7. What opportunities are you creating to help quieter students explore their own passions and interests?

CHAPTER 3
THE CONDITIONS FOR
COMMUNICATION

Mr Pessimistico is having one of his daily staffroom rants. Miss Honey, the department's NQT, is cowering behind a gigantic stack of books, but still he seeks her out. He is wielding his class list and gesticulating wildly: "This lad, James Marshall. Have you come across him? I have no idea what to do with him. He is just so quiet, I can't get him to say anything in lessons at all. There just seems to be nothing upstairs with that boy!"

In staffrooms across the land, frustrations are being voiced over students' reluctance to take part in discussions. Variations on the rant are subtle: we might bemoan a lack of "spark" or we might define individuals, or indeed whole groups of students, as "too passive". And despite how the rant might sound, at heart the intentions are good.

Students like this exist in every class. They seem to want the ground to swallow them up every time we engage with them. Nothing we do encourages them to volunteer answers and that fills us with guilt. We feel a professional obligation to help these reticent young people to find their voices, to grow in confidence so they are ready to face the challenges the world will throw at them. It appears to us to be a poor reflection on our teaching, or indeed our ability to form effective relationships, that they are not leaping forward to express themselves. Perhaps more cynically, we are also aware of how the situation may look to outside observers: their lack of input means they can appear disengaged.

Yet should we really be defining engagement as verbal input into lessons? Are other forms of participation not equally valid, like writing and listening?

Under pressure

In 2013, *The Atlantic* magazine published an article entitled "Introverted Kids Need to Learn to Speak Up at School". The standfirst read: "Every child should be graded on class participation – and parents don't help their children when they argue otherwise." In the article, the teacher Jessica Lahey wrote: "It is my job to teach grammar, vocabulary, and literature, but I must also teach my students how to succeed in the world we live in – a world where most people won't stop talking. If anything, I feel even more strongly that my introverted students must learn how to self-advocate by communicating with parents, educators, and the world at large."

This belief – that there is an urgent need to instil extrovert qualities in introverted students in order to help them "succeed" – is common in education. There is no denying that students face pressure to speak up and contribute in the classroom and elsewhere. This pressure comes from a range of sources: from parents who want their children to do well; from teachers who want to hear students' perspectives; and from peers who make it look so easy. Thus, there is a focus on extrovert forms of participation, rather than reflection and inner dialogue.

Interestingly, in infant classes, if children are asked "Did you enjoy working in a group?" in an extravagant tone by their teacher, they will sense how important it is to answer in the affirmative and nod accordingly. In contrast, if they are asked "What did you like? What did you not like?", then they are given the freedom to share their true feelings and reactions. They are therefore able to grow in an emotionally connected environment where diverse views and differing strengths are accepted and acknowledged.

This is even more important when one realises that many introverted children live under the tyranny of imagined consequences – they are more likely to ask "what if?" than their more extroverted peers. Children flourish in known environments with just the right amount of challenge. If overwhelmed with what ifs, they may fall into patterns of behaviour to self-soothe and stay in their comfort zone. This is another reminder of why the early nursery and school experience is crucial, and why careful and sustained teaching of emotional intelligence and resilience is paramount.

Quietly disengaged?
Forcing students to talk when they are not prepared, or when they have little to say, can only damage their confidence. We have already reflected on the tremendous power of teachers to influence the emotional state of students, and this is particularly strong during moments of classroom dialogue.

The culture of classroom talk begins in nursery/infant classes, with "show and tell" or with children sharing what they got up to when the class teddy bear stayed with them for the weekend. Yet, even after such early experiences, many young people detest giving talks and presentations.

The answer is not to avoid classroom talk altogether, but instead to find ways to gradually build resilience and confidence. We all need to present to others in life, and the self-esteem gained when fears are overcome can be life-changing for children (and adults too!). Young people are not merely empty vessels to be filled with knowledge and they should not be allowed to fall into patterns of passive non-compliance. They should be inspired to consider how best they can make progress and grow to be adult participants in our world.

The reflections of a retired primary teacher who wished to remain anonymous illustrate just how challenging this can be:

> "Probably the thing that I am proudest of as a teacher is that quiet children were happy being taught by me (according to their parents). I think they felt safe in that they were not going to be pushed into uncomfortable situations too soon. It is a time thing and not a quick fix.
>
> I can now stand up and speak in front of a roomful of people – I couldn't possibly as a child. In secondary school my reports were good, but spoilt in my eyes by the continual comment that I needed to take an active part, as if I could just read it and think 'must start speaking'! It actually makes you far more self-conscious.
>
> I remember once when something exciting had happened and with my friend I was recounting it to a teacher and then my friend took over. The teacher immediately asked her to let me finish and at that point I realised she wasn't interested in what we were saying – it was the fact I was saying it. Very inhibiting so I didn't say anything further. It would have been so much better had she let my friend continue and then I would have added more. I suppose the main thing I am saying is: don't draw attention to the fact that someone is quiet – it is counter-productive. Give an environment where they feel confident enough to speak."

The first step towards building confidence in quieter students is learning to understand each individual and why they might be more reticent; next comes sensitive encouragement and support. Always bear in mind that there is a link between emotional competence and achievement.

So, how do we create an environment that builds confidence? First we need to consider the purpose of communication in our classrooms.

Why communicate?

To suggest that we teach in silence would be ludicrous. Students need to feel that classrooms are rich in dialogue and discussion, whether or not they contribute verbally. There needs to be an expectation that they are reflecting and developing – being pushed just outside their comfort zone in order to grow. We must all feel comfortable, as lifelong learners, to innovate and take risks without the threat of being punished if we fail.

So, why does communication exist in classrooms? And how can we convey these reasons to students simply and efficiently? A discussion in which students offer their own perspectives on why discussions take place is a useful starting point, and this can be supported by our own input. Here are the key purposes of discussion presented in a simple list:

- To help teachers check for understanding.
- To help develop confidence in public speaking.
- To develop our ability to learn from each other.
- To externalise and help make our thinking clear.
- To build positive relationships.

Once students understand the reasons for discussion, we can try out various ways of eliciting contributions from them all.

Sensitive encouragement

Sensitivity and empathy are necessary qualities of any effective teacher. They can be the difference between a young person feeling comfortable in the classroom or feeling such anxiety that learning is impossible. Without them, we are left in the situation outlined by the psychologist Barbara Markway in her book *Painfully Shy: How to Overcome Social Anxiety and Reclaim Your Life*: "I still remember one horrible day in high school when a math teacher called attention to my quietness. He told the whole class that I was the quietest student he'd ever had in his twenty-two years of teaching. Of course, everyone turned around to look at me, as if I was some kind of freak. I was humiliated and felt deep shame. I truly believed there was something wrong with me. It didn't even cross my mind that there was something wrong with a teacher who would make such a statement."

Managing classroom dialogue is one way in which teachers' interpersonal skills are put to the test. We should always strive to scaffold and support students' ability to communicate – the practical discussion strategies offered in the next chapter can help.

Talk about it

How often do we explore the idea of discussion with our students? We might set some boundaries or guidelines at the start of an academic year, but they often relate to the basics of how discussion operates in the classroom.

Examining who talks and when is a deeper, equally important conversation. Considering why some young people are more inclined to share ideas and volunteer answers is the first step towards celebrating the diversity of our students. It can be as simple as recognising that whereas some people want to think out loud, others don't.

Talking about how this can make students feel is very healthy: by vocalising the fact that discussion can make some students anxious, we can begin to normalise those emotions. Being given permission to be quieter and more thoughtful might just help our introverted students to feel less pressure. And for the students who share openly and regularly, pointing out the differences between personalities might help them to hone some of the quieter, more reflective skills that we will explore later.

It is important to examine the need for quiet in lessons and how silence can help young people to think. In music lessons, children are taught from a young age that silence is crucial: it is how we create rhythm; it is how we listen and respond. Bring this into your classroom – sound and silence are both vital to the whole.

Katherine Schultz, the author of *Rethinking Classroom Participation: Listening to Silent Voices*, provides a series of useful questions: "Can students participate without speaking out loud? Should teachers consider the times that a student gives silent assent to a question or thoughtfully jots notes for a future essay as participation? Are these useful forms of participation? It is important to note that one student's silence can enable another student to speak. Do students have a responsibility to contribute to the silence of a classroom so that others can talk, along with a responsibility to contribute verbally to the discussion? How might silence be re-framed as a 'productive' or useful contribution to participation in classrooms?"

We will return to these essential questions later. Sharing such thinking with students is a powerful tool, as is giving them the opportunity to reflect on how they participate in lessons.

Time to reflect

Given how much time whole-class dialogue and question-and-answer sessions take up in lessons, it is important to encourage all students to consider how they contribute in these situations. Doing this collectively as a class, rather than individually, can alleviate the pressure that some students may feel. They can write down their reflections on this issue, rather than feeling they have to vocalise sensitive thoughts in front of their peers.

Students can then be encouraged to set dialogue targets, ones as simple as trying to raise their hand once in a lesson and slowly increasing their contributions. Try these questions to stretch students' thinking:

- How comfortable are you contributing in front of the whole class?

- How regularly do you share your thoughts?

- What kind of dialogue and discussion are you most comfortable with?

- What prevents you from contributing? What can you do about this?

Returning to these questions periodically keeps the exploration of discussion and dialogue alive in classrooms.

Quality, not quantity

In all walks of life, the myth pervades that those who talk the most or the loudest are the most intelligent. We all have students who leap to answer every question and talk as much as possible. Finding subtle ways to challenge this and encourage quality responses, rather than lots of responses, can make life easier for our quiet students. Celebrating perceptive and thoughtful answers by offering genuine praise can also encourage others to extend their thinking.

Classroom ethos

The ethos we present to our students around verbal contributions is hugely significant. As we encourage students to value quality over quantity, we should also seek to validate the effort and thinking that goes into volunteering answers. Praise will be unpicked in the next chapter, but letting students know how much we appreciate it when they share their thoughts will make sure they feel valued enough to continue contributing.

The attitude we have towards mistakes matters greatly to our students. Do we belittle and scorn, or do we seek to celebrate errors and use them as learning opportunities? In order to establish an atmosphere of respect in the classroom, teachers and students should follow these rules during discussion:

- **Focus on the speaker**. Make sure students show eye contact to all those who contribute verbally in the classroom, whether a teacher or a peer.

- **No interruptions**. This is essential if we are to encourage all young people to share openly. There is nothing worse for a quieter student who has finally taken the step to share than being drowned out by noise. If another student wishes to challenge or give their views, coach them in an "excuse me" style of interruption.

- **Sensitive feedback**. Guiding students in how they respond to their peers is challenging but important. Teachers can model how to be specific, respectful and clear, and provide plenty of opportunities for practice.

A culture of fear does nothing to help our quiet students. But emphasising that everyone is unique and everyone matters can encourage more introverted students to contribute. There are also practical steps we can take to manage classroom interactions – we will explore these in chapter 3…

A quiet reflection

Joe Moran (@joemoransblog) is a professor of English and cultural history at Liverpool John Moores University. He is the author of a range of nonfiction books, including Shrinking Violets: The Secret Life of Shyness *and* First You Write a Sentence: The Elements of Reading, Writing … and Life.

Some people might think it odd that a shy person like me should have been drawn to a profession, teaching, that involves so much social performance and interaction. In fact, I have found that shy teachers are often very able performers. My big fear in normal conversation is that I am boring my interlocutor, which makes me throw away my words and trail off at the end of sentences, so the fear becomes self-fulfilling. But in front of a class I have been given permission to speak uninterrupted, and am free to make up a slightly amplified, cartoonish version of myself.

I am also reassured by clarity and structure, by physical props that tell me how I should behave. When I have my notes in front of me and a clicker in my hand, I know I have been given a second chance to impersonate a normal person, in the same way that shy police officers or shy train managers are said to be emboldened by wearing a uniform. In a world where we have to pretend that most of our performances are natural, one that does not hide its status as such feels like a deliverance. German has a word for it: *Maskenfreiheit*, the freedom that comes from wearing masks.

I try to bear this in mind when teaching shy students. I teach English, a discussion-based subject, and many of my students run the gamut from mild shyness to the extreme social anxiety that makes it hard for them even to be in class. I know from experience that if a shy student hasn't spoken in class for several weeks, it gets harder for them the longer they leave it (because what they then might say will seem to carry huge significance). So I try to give them a chance to speak early on in some rehearsed way – either by asking them to prepare something or giving them a heads-up that I'm going to ask them a question. This might sound daunting but my hope is that shy students like being given permission to speak.

I used simply to be relieved that I could get students talking in class, that I had conjured up a discussion that lasted the requisite time. Nowadays I tend to leave longer silences after asking questions and not worry too much about creating a contrived chattiness. I hope, as part of an English degree, that I can teach my students how to talk and write well. But I want also to leave them with a salutary sense of the limits of language, a recognition that we can never make ourselves wholly understood with these slippery, better-than-nothing things called words. Such an awareness, that communicating with each other is hard and often fails, might make us listen and talk better.

In a world of constant babble and blather, I hope that such slightly awkward silences might inspire in my students a thoughtfulness about how much can be known and how much we really understand each other. An English class could be, if nothing else, a break from the endless noise of the endlessly mediatised lives of young people – a brief respite from being constantly available to others via those familiar dancing thumbs on a touchscreen. It could be a replenishing pause – a space to stop, breathe and think.

More and more I'm drawn to the idea of a class as being like Quaker worship – a place of silence and shared attention. Quakers meet in plain, unadorned rooms and sit facing each other. There are no pulpits, because all are meant to be equal before God, and no set prayers, readings or hymns. The meeting starts as soon as the first person enters the room, and it begins with people sat in silence. Then someone might stand up and share something with those present. After this, the group returns to silence. Quakers believe, along with the playwright Eugène Ionesco, that "words stop silence from speaking". The words puncture the silence rather than the other way round. This means that, when words intervene in the silence, they should matter.

I think of an English class as a cure for that state of permanent distraction that makes it hard for us to properly talk and listen to each other. True articulacy, which is being able to string sentences together in a way that acknowledges the existence of a listener, is a virtuoso skill. This is what I try to teach – because if anyone should know that conversation is a hard-to-master art, it is a shy teacher.

Introspection

1. Do you criticise quiet students for their lack of contribution?

2. Do you place undue pressure on students to contribute often?

3. What other forms of contribution could you begin to prioritise in your lessons?

4. How often do you talk carefully about contribution rates and discussions?

5. How often do you give students time to reflect on their classroom dialogue?

6. Are you messaging positivity about silence and reflection, and about quality over quantity?

CHAPTER 4 STRATEGIES FOR COMMUNICATION

Joseph is in biology. It is period five and, as is often the case, he has not contributed verbally in today's lessons. The teacher, Mrs Rapido, is introducing the concept of osmosis.

Despite never having explored this with the class, she asks the question, "What do I mean by osmosis?" She scans the faces of 30 apathetic adolescents, then seeks out Joseph. "Can you give me a definition, Joseph?" He looks up, perplexed, his face signalling a complete blank. She pauses, then says, "No, anyone else? No?"

This is Joseph's only whole-class interaction of the day.

Meaningful discussions are the bedrock of effective classroom learning. In the ideal educational world, our lessons would be packed with open-ended and deep discussions in which we grappled with complex topics. Far too often, however, discussions descend into awkwardness, or consist of grunted and monosyllabic answers. Or, in the other extreme, they are dominated by a core group of extroverted students, with the majority as semi-observant passengers.

The classroom ethos and the interpersonal dynamic, as outlined in the previous chapter, have a significant impact on the quality of communication. Alongside this are subtle teaching adjustments we can make in order to improve dialogue and support communication. The first is a simple change to how we use time in lessons.

One of the reasons why classroom discussions can create stress for students is the speed at which they are expected to generate ideas. Teachers tend to demand responses at a pace that would be unnatural in any other setting. Inevitably, these rapid-fire questioning strategies elicit only underdeveloped answers and compound the anxiety that students may be feeling. Although urgency and direction are important in any classroom, all students will on occasion need more time to process information.

The introvert brain

This space for thinking is particularly important for quieter and more introverted students. The way in which introverts process information means that they, more than their extroverted peers, need time to think before they speak. In her book *The Introvert Advantage: How Quiet People Can Thrive in an Extrovert World*, the psychotherapist Marti Olsen Laney suggests that brain chemistry differs markedly between introverts and extroverts. Neural pathways in introverts are longer and more complex, thus it takes them longer to process information.

Our classroom environments should therefore enable time to think through ideas. As we shall see in a later chapter, deep focus is what we want all students to strive for. Building in "wait time" is a simple way to improve the thinking that takes place in lessons and hone the ability of students to remain present and focused.

Wait time

Mary Budd Rowe was an American educator who published pioneering research on the idea of "wait time" in the 1970s. This revealed the impact of allowing three to five seconds in which students could reflect before answering a question. Wait time taps into the way a quieter student's mind works, but it has numerous benefits for all young people.

Consider these words from Rowe: "There are increases in the length of the response, the number of unsolicited appropriate responses, student confidence, incidence of speculative responses, incidence of child-child data comparisons, incidence of evidence-inference statements, frequency of student questions, and incidence of responses from 'relatively slow' students. The number of teacher questions which do not elicit a response decreases."

Pressing pause in a lesson does not come particularly naturally to teachers and will initially be greeted with odd looks from students. Like any classroom strategy, however, with regular practice it becomes more natural – for us and for them. Explain to students that this time will be left and why. Then count internally to five before you request an answer – at first it can feel like an eternity.

This strategy might not be appropriate for all questions, particularly when it comes to factual recall. But for more conceptual questions – the how and why that require deeper reflection – leaving time for processing can be very effective. Try the following phrases to help establish this strategy in your classroom:

- I am going to give you some time to reflect on that more challenging question.

- I will give you some time to think through your answer to that question.

- Take a few seconds and consider how you might phrase your answer.

- I will be asking two students to respond after some time to consider.

Students, however, are masters at acting in the way they think we want them to. Thinking time will result in faces that are a picture of profound philosophical consideration, but they are often masks that have been perfected through years of learned behaviour in the classroom. What we need to do is coach students in how they might reflect during this pause.

We don't want them to use this opportunity to drift off into thoughts of last night's *Call of Duty* battle. What we do want is for them to begin framing their answers in their minds and weighing up possible options – I call this the "internal verbal". And if you want to extend the thinking time, students can try a "paired verbal" with another member of the class. Teachers can use ideas like this to keep the experience of reflection fresh, but students also need to have an understanding of expectations and how to share their feedback in stages. This helps to make discussion and dialogue feel natural in a class environment, and begins to reduce stress among quieter students.

Over time, even the most extroverted students, the ones who dive straight into dialogue without forethought, will recognise why it is helpful to think through their answers in advance. The result is what we are all striving for: classrooms in which reflection and thinking are rich.

Early participation

On Susan Cain's website Quiet Revolution (quietrev.com), the teacher John Spencer writes the following: "As a student, I was an eager hand-raiser. I spoke up. I shared my opinions. I wasn't particularly quiet. Inside, though, I was terrified. I didn't want to be caught off-guard, forced to share my thoughts to an entire class without having the chance to think through things on my own. For this reason, I developed a strategy. When a teacher first started talking about a particular topic, I'd jot down five of the best questions I could conjure up. I would rehearse them in my head until the words sounded right. This allowed me to speak up without being put on the spot."

This is an interesting insight into the sinking feeling we get when we feel everyone around us has contributed something useful to a discussion, while we haven't yet spoken. Panic and insecurity set in. Our thinking is constricted by anxiety and any hope of contributing usefully to the discussion is lost.

This all-too-frequent experience in adult meetings is, of course, an example of what life can be like for young people in the classroom. What we perhaps don't appreciate, however, is that their every school day involves the complex human interplay of a large meeting for six or seven hours. For some, this can be exhausting.

There will be students for whom this sinking feeling grows as a lesson continues. We can help to keep such emotions in check and build confidence by giving them an opportunity to take part early on. There are various ways to enable this. One is to use Doug Lemov's cold-call strategy from *Teach Like a Champion*, calling on a more reticent student to answer a question at the beginning of a lesson. Start with a question that is easier and more related to recall, giving them the confidence that they can answer correctly.

Susan Cain suggests discussing this with the student in advance, explaining that getting in early with an answer will help to boost their confidence: "Both parents and teachers can work with a child one-on-one, offering strategies for participation – such as offering a comment early in class, before anticipatory anxiety grows too strong." Then you can deliver feedback that recognises this is a significant step for the student, helping them to feel they can continue to participate in lessons.

The power of praise

How we praise our quieter students can be transformative in terms of confidence and relationships. Extroverts are more likely to thrive on being publicly lauded and recognised for their work. We can, in fact, reinforce extroverted norms in the classroom by over-praising quick responses and simple answers, rather than the thoughtful and extended answers we wish to hear more often.

Introverted students may require more nuanced forms of praise. A quiet piece of feedback can really help to foster confidence. This is one of the absolute delights of teaching: when we make the space and time to offer sincere and personalised praise to a student. When their face lights up, we are reminded of what our core business is: to encourage and inspire young people to want to achieve more.

All it takes is a quick one-to-one conversation at the end of a lesson, or perhaps a written comment in their book that validates their effort. A brief email to parents or a phone call home can also be brilliant ways to build a student's confidence.

Raising hands

One of the most obvious signals of extroversion in the classroom is a hand going up to volunteer an answer. It is the most visible sign of a desire to communicate and it indicates a level of confidence.

There is no doubt that students raising their hands will always be a part of lessons – banishing it from classrooms would be hugely limiting for teachers and would remove the opportunity for young people to demonstrate knowledge or even show enthusiasm. Yet, for some of our students, the mere act of raising a hand is a significant step.

So, rather than ending the practice altogether, perhaps we need to make more judicious use of raising hands to volunteer answers. Instead of seeking hands for every answer, we could ask a question and be clear that we don't want hands to be raised. If we do seek hands, we could count the number of hands we have, then encourage more time for thinking. This gives quieter students the opportunity to begin formulating an answer internally. It also removes some of the competitiveness, as students don't need to rush to be the first to raise their hand. Again, it is helpful to introduce this strategy in advance:

- This is a hands-free question.

- I appreciate you might want to raise your hands for this question, but I am going to nominate some answers.

- Let's try hands-down for this question.

- For the next ten minutes, hands-up is banned!

Read the room

An essential and under-discussed area of teaching is our capacity to "read the room". Our awareness and understanding of our students can help us to gauge who is keen to contribute. Look for facial feedback and other cues that suggest a student might like the opportunity to share a thoughtful response. One of my favourite lines of classroom dialogue is "I can see it your eyes!" – this tells students that you believe they have the answer in them. More often than not, this gives them confidence and encourages them to share.

The issue is, of course, that restricting the use of hand-raising can place extra pressure on more introverted students, who won't know if you are planning to pick them to answer. So, it is important for this to be coupled with the wait-time strategies explored earlier. Building in time for students to discuss their thoughts with a peer will also help; this discussion needs to be clearly structured to ensure it is meaningful, and students must know who you expect to answer and how.

Pair-share

A seating arrangement is a powerful tool in helping our quieter students to feel more comfortable. And if they are sitting alongside someone they feel comfortable with, then we can make greater use of the pair-share activity. This caters for both introverts and extroverts: introverts can have a quieter, more focused conversation that feels less overwhelming than a group situation; extroverts have the opportunity to instantly vocalise their thinking.

Pair-share also gives teachers time to circulate the room and note any misconceptions. The conditions in which pair-share dialogue takes place are, of course, important and require student training. Young people need to be reminded to "box" themselves in with their partner and not let the dialogue extend to others around them. And the conversation has to stay on-topic – another reason why our circulating around the room is necessary.

Write it down

At times, you may want students to reflect on something internally and carefully. Give them an appropriate length of time and the necessary quiet to allow for real conceptional thinking, then ask them to write down an answer before vocalising it. This will help them to construct a solid argument that they feel more confident in sharing.

Mini whiteboards can also help you to manage dialogue in lessons. Ask your students to write down and then hold up their answer to a question. In this way there is no insecurity to overcome, as all the students are in the same position. Use a signal word so they all show you their answers at the same time, otherwise it is once again the triumph of the more competitive extroverts in the room!

Student questions

Allowing time for students to formulate their own questions not only develops more inquisitive mindsets, but also helps quieter students to express themselves. It gives them a chance to make sense of the thoughts that may be bouncing around in their minds, as well as the repeated refrain of "what if?" that they may be experiencing.

By asking students to write down questions at various points in the lesson, perhaps on a Post-it note, we can gain an insight into just how reflective and self-aware some of our less verbally expressive students are. This can be done individually, but it can also be an interesting task for students to complete in pairs or in groups. They can return to these notes when they revisit the topic at a later date, when more time can be built in for quiet reflection.

Space to think

The physical proximity of their classmates can make it hard for quieter students to find space in their minds to reflect. Noise and frequent chatter can compress the brain and leave them feeling overstimulated. If we consider the amount of stimulus experienced by our quieter students, then it is clear why they may wish to slip into anonymity during class discussions. In secondary schools, students bounce from subject to subject, interacting with a range of peers, and even more social interaction is required at break times and lunchtimes. School means noise, stimulus and overcrowding.

The physical act of moving from one classroom to another helps students to clear space in their brains for the next lesson, but it is important to be aware of where your students have come from. Liaising with support staff, who are with classes regularly, can help you to meet the needs of young people who may be reaching information overload. Pupil support assistants have valuable knowledge of students – crucially, across lessons we do not see.

A designated thinking area in a classroom, where children can go to find space and calm, can be very useful (this may be more appropriate in primary schools). Reading zones can also be helpful. Even allowing students to use your classroom at lunchtime can offer them some respite from the intensity of the day.

This chapter's strategies can help to keep dialogue focused and improve participation, but the controversy surrounding collaboration and group work has been deliberately avoided. This is not because group work shouldn't be a part of lessons, but rather because it needs very skilful management in order to be positive. We will delve into that conundrum in the next chapter.

A quiet reflection

Aidan Severs (@thatboycanteach) is a primary school deputy headteacher. He runs thatboycanteach.co.uk

As a self-diagnosed ambivert, I imagine that I have some level of insight into the experiences of both introverts and extroverts. My main observation with regards to education is that schools do not seem to be places which naturally favour introversion, in students or in teachers. But I don't think that has to be the case.

Let's take teachers for a start. More introverted teachers do exist, probably contrary to popular belief. Not all teachers are the wisecracking, larger-than-life characters that we imagine a good teacher should be. And probably they'll be the teachers who get feedback about their "classroom presence" and whose development points might as well be "be more like the teacher next door".

And this is where the plight of the introverted teacher is actually just a microcosm of a much wider problem: there is often very little allowance for personality in teaching. We might have just got over the idea of an "Ofsted lesson" (which, by extension, always needed to be taught by an "Ofsted teacher") but every teacher is potentially at the mercy of a leader who wants things done in a certain way.

Leaders must be ready to allow introverted teachers to be themselves. If their classroom management is lacking, then how can they be developed without advice that amounts to "be more extroverted"? If they don't speak up in meetings, then find a better forum for them to have a voice. If they need some space at lunchtime instead of joining in the staffroom banter, then leave them be to manage their own time in a way that allows them to get back in the classroom to do their job.

And our introverted students need introverted teachers. In an environment that prizes loud, brash, outgoing types, they need to see that success doesn't only come from being gregarious. If we allow introverted teachers to be successful and evidently introverted, then the one in three students who are introverted will have a positive role model.

These teachers will also have a much better insight into how to treat the more obviously introverted students. The number of times I've read reports and heard parents being told that their child needs to say more in class suggests a belief that speaking out in front of 30 people is a necessary life skill. It also suggests something more serious: that some teachers don't realise that what they are looking for is just a proxy for learning.

Just because a student can't verbalise it, that doesn't mean they haven't learnt it. The same if they can't discuss it in a large group. Yes, it might be easier for a teacher to assess a student by such contributions – after all, speaking one-to-one to 30 different students, or setting a written task that requires hours of marking, is very time-consuming for the teacher. But that can't be the reason why we expect students to just cast aside their natural tendency towards introversion.

That's not to say that we shouldn't help more introverted students to develop skills which come more naturally to extroverts. No introvert believes that public speaking, spending more time with people, or working collaboratively are bad things, or abilities that they don't need or want. We should help students to develop these skills, but with realistic expectations based on their tendencies.

But, more importantly than that, we should be celebrating all the positives that introverted people, teachers and students alike, quite naturally possess: slow, more deliberate and more thoughtful working habits; the desire to focus on one task at a time; the desire to devote social energies to deeper relationships; the ability to listen rather than talk and to think before they speak; the wish to avoid unnecessary conflict. They're all pretty good qualities to possess, if you ask me. If schools, and indeed the world, were run by more introverts it wouldn't be a bad thing!

Introspection

1. Are your lessons dominated by a handful of confident individuals?

2. Do you leave enough time for thinking and reflection?

3. Is there scope for students to formulate questions in your lessons?

4. What pair-share strategies could you make greater use of?

5. Can you create opportunities for students to record answers in writing before being expected to give verbal answers?

CHAPTER 5
ON COLLABORATION

Harry and his class have been delving into the causes of the First World War in their history lessons. In this particular lesson, they are exploring the alliance system and how it contributed to the conflict. The students are watching a short clip explaining the two different alliances. Mrs Grouper stops the clip and says, "Right, I would like you to now get into your groups of six and discuss how important you think the alliances were in causing the war."

Harry looks around at his peers as they instantly begin discussing last night's football match. Skilled in the art of going undetected, they quickly change the subject when Mrs Grouper approaches their desk.

If I had a penny for every time group work, collaboration and discussion were mentioned in my teacher training, I would be considerably richer than I am now. As hardly the most discerning of educational customers, I became a group-work evangelist. In my early observations of learning, I would scoff at lessons that contained little group work: no roaming students, no extended dialogue in groups? I would watch the clock when a teacher was talking and feel genuine horror if they spoke for longer than a minute.

When I was eventually let loose on unsuspecting teenagers, I puzzled over why behaviour worsened after my protracted group-work sessions. I would peer anxiously at the outcomes in student books and wonder why none of those wonderful collaborative moments translated into anything meaningful.

These days, group work is no longer promoted quite so zealously. Individual lesson experiences are not subject to the same level of scrutiny and judgement, and the growing consensus is that group work doesn't in fact need to be at the heart of every lesson. But that is not to say that group work is redundant – far from it. Young people, now more than ever, need to be trained in social skills and group dynamics. As with any pedagogical practice, however, group work needs to be carefully orchestrated and planned in order to have a positive impact on learning.

When we make quiet students our focus, it becomes obvious that group work is problematic. We have seen that introverted students are prone to sensory overload and may seek anonymity in a group dynamic. They are most comfortable in calm, low-key environments. In group situations, the likelihood of them not contributing is high. So our careful attempts to nurture and build their confidence may be undone unless we avoid some of the common pitfalls of group work.

Group-work traps

There is much that can go wrong with group work – I bear the scars of many failed experiments. Breakdowns in behaviour and communication were common in my early attempts to use group work in lessons. We have all seen it happen: students are left to their own devices for too long and their focus drifts spectacularly. The lesson time is completely wasted – the students would have learned more working independently. Considering the amount of time that group work can take to structure and facilitate, this can be intensely frustrating.

Unstructured group tasks also provide the ideal place for power and personality dynamics to be played out. The confident individuals who dominate discussion in lessons take complete control of the group. The quieter students fade into the background. The lazier students sit back, yawn and switch off. This does nothing to challenge social norms in the classroom. And, unless we know our students well, it is hard to discern between those who are quiet and those who are lazy.

Another concern may be the quality of the thinking that occurs within groups. *The Organization Man*, William H Whyte's influential book on management from 1956, is interesting in this regard: "The most misguided attempt at false collectivization is the current attempt to see the group as a creative vehicle … People very rarely *think* in groups; they talk together, they exchange information, they adjudicate, they make compromises. But they do not think; they do not create."

But this is not another polemic about how group work should be consigned to the pedagogical dustbin. Instead, I want to explore how we can make it effective and make it work for quieter students.

Benefits of group work

In our society, professionally at least, we are not wholly autonomous. Instead, we are expected to collaborate: to work closely with others and to arrive at outcomes as harmoniously as possible. To deny young people the chance to develop these skills would be to fail to prepare them for the world outside the classroom.

It is our responsibility as teachers to provide opportunities for group discussion and decision-making. We all need people to help draw out our ideas and encourage us to improve, and group work can be a way for students to share their expertise and abilities. It also allows us to coach them in debating and challenging ideas appropriately – skills that, as we shall see, need to be modelled by us. If done particularly well, group work can enable intense focus, concentration and effort – effort that might go beyond what each member of the group could produce on their own.

We also want to help students develop the communication skills they will need when they leave school. Structured opportunities for group discussion can teach them to adjust their style and method of communication for different audiences and purposes. Group work can also cultivate self-awareness among young people, giving them a better understanding of themselves and how they function in group settings.

Perhaps the most obvious reason for group work is the need for variation. Students – and teachers – need changes of pace to keep them interested, and group activities can lift a lesson that might have been heavily teacher-led. All our attention spans can be re-energised by a short, well-planned group task. For quieter students, group work can be designed to build confidence and interpersonal skills. It can also give their more extroverted classmates the chance to recognise and appreciate the skills of others.

Your expectations

Placing young people in large groups without clear guidelines for behaviour is unlikely to result in the desired outcome. We need to be completely clear with students about our expectations for the interpersonal dynamic.

Below, I set out three important areas for discussion with students: good listening, appropriate challenge and encouraging participation. These skills are key to any professional environment, so students need to learn them. Of course, we teachers strive to model these in our own classroom interactions, but to really bring the message home we need to make these implicit skills as explicit as possible for students:

1. **What constitutes good listening?** Given how often students are asked to listen, it is odd that significantly more time is not invested in honing their ability to listen with intent and respect. This should be a ubiquitous conversation in classrooms: what are the qualities of good listening? A chapter is devoted to this later in the book.

2. **How do we challenge each other?** Group work arguably works best when there is something for students to debate. Put the following phrases on a PowerPoint slide or a sheet to help students discuss emotive issues constructively and respectfully:

- I agree to an extent, however…

- In my view…

- I would challenge that statement…

- I would offer an alternative…

- Yes, but have you considered…

3. **How do we encourage participation?** Drawing out the views of others – rather than just outlining our own opinion – is a nuanced skill that is refined as we grow older. Coaching students in how to do this will lead to more successful group tasks.

We also need to consider the outcome of the activity. What exactly do we want students to produce in the time permitted? Sharing this with them will prevent any confusion, ensuring that each member of the group knows exactly what they are working towards.

Structure it

What is the purpose of the group activity? How does it reinforce the aims of the lesson? Once we are clear on this, we can provide clarity for our students about the learning intention. We then need to structure the following areas:

- **Timing.** How much time will they have for the task? The maximum time we can expect students to work effectively on a group activity is 15 minutes. Provide a break in the middle of longer group tasks.

- **Responsibility.** What are the necessary roles and which students are going to perform them? This needs to be carefully mapped out and shared with the group beforehand. Of course, it is important to consider students' different characteristics and skills.

- **Feedback.** How are the groups going to share the results of the task and who will be responsible for delivering the feedback?

A moment to reflect

An important theme of this book is allowing space and time for quiet reflection, so that students develop the metacognitive skills to understand their strengths and weaknesses (more on this later). Group work needs to be followed with time to think and make sense of the material explored. Switching from the high stimulus of group conversation to the silence of contemplative reflection also allows students to recharge their batteries.

This period of reflection can be driven by a series of questions asked by the teacher, or students can come up with the questions themselves. It allows a state of calm to return to the classroom and acts as a bridge to the next part of the lesson.

Quiet voices

It is vital that we play to the strengths of introverted students in group work. Unless this is considered carefully, they may struggle to navigate the social dynamics and their voices may go unheard. At times it may be appropriate to let students choose who they work with: if they feel comfortable with the group they will be more likely to contribute.

Assigning each group member a defined role can help to prevent the more dominant personalities from overpowering the quieter ones. In the role of note-taker or scribe, for example, quieter young people can use their listening skills for the benefit of the group. And it is important for the teacher to circulate, modelling how to include others in discussion.

Remember to repeat the message that group work will help to hone their communication skills over time. I also share my experiences of group discussion tasks in job interviews (in which I have often performed dreadfully) and the fact that many organisations now include these as part of their selection criteria.

In the next chapter we will consider the complete opposite of noisy group work: silence. How can we use silence to bring out the best in our quieter students? And how can it help all young people to focus and think more deeply?

A quiet reflection

During my research for this book, I spoke to a wide range of young people. Their views on the efficacy of group work were particularly interesting. Ellie Rensner wrote this thoughtful piece on the pros and cons of group work when she was 16.

What do we need? Another teaching method suited exclusively to extroverts? A method by which we can grow and support each other, all the while absorbing our vital maths and English skills? It appears ideal, but unfortunately there seems to be a price to pay for the supposedly revolutionary learning method of "the group project" – and that price is our solitude. We trade in our quiet isolation for boisterous calamity and a scramble of conflicting ideas. But perhaps that is the most efficient technique for extroverts, even if it is devastating for introverts. If this is the case, then how do we satisfy both?

From personal experience in present-day classrooms, it is apparent that group work is the newest infatuation. Most teachers will jump at any chance to throw us into groups and set us off on an exciting project – a task which could be completed quite adequately without the disturbance of your "team mates", but which nonetheless we must power through together.

We must, through the magic of teamwork and communication, produce the greatest ideas and achieve the highest grades possible, all while making friendships to last a lifetime. Seems like an unfaultable plan. How could you fail? You have the awe-inspiring power of group work and conversation to guide you through to the best possible outcome.

However, this is, of course, not in the least bit realistic. Most of these groups (cleverly constructed to ensure you are mixed together with the people you are most uncomfortable with) are highly inefficient. Typically, one or two of the loudest group members will take over, leaving the quieter outcasts to be left unheard. They cannot benefit from this exercise in the same way the loud children do. The group will either be taken over or the opposite will occur – group members will not participate. The scene of a group of mismatched students sat awkwardly around a desk in silence is a scene known all too well.

Likewise, the scene of all group members sat in uncomfortable hush while one panicked student scrambles desperately to churn out some kind of idea is, again, known all too well. In every group situation it is practically a guarantee that one, or several, of the group members will not engage, leaving it down to one or two distressed students to figure it out.

When this happens the children will tend to copy others' ideas and forget their own. Students who are keen to learn and achieve are held back, and the poor work eventually produced reflects badly on them. And they have no control over it. In this way the whole ideology behind group work – that it is there to allow you to produce your best work through collaboration – backfires, but, alas, there is no way to stop this from happening. There will always be students who just don't care and will not cooperate.

While many students may opt for group work – purely as they know it is the most likely way to ensure they have to do as little work as possible – it certainly does not work for a large number of people. Research indicates that when left to work alone away from influence, people are more creative.

Studies by psychologists Mihaly Csikszentmihalyi and Gregory Feist show that highly creative people in many fields are often introverted. Introverts are much more comfortable working alone. In fact, introverts require quiet and isolation to produce their best work. If given privacy they are more constructive. Solitude allows us to learn.

Years of research shows us that when it comes to quality and quantity of work, individuals almost always will work better than groups. The more group members there are only results in a worse performance. Work is just not all about talking. As well as healthy discussions and idea sharing, we need room to think things over and to clarify our own ideas. It is argued that group work is crucial in preparing you for similar life situations and this is true to an extent. However, in schools we should also allow children to work and learn alone, without influence or disruption.

All that said, group work, of course, does have its benefits (even if few). Group work can be fun and stimulating. It can be an effective way to swap ideas. Yet perhaps it is more beneficial for younger children. As we have progressed into high school, group projects seem to be less popular (maybe we owe this to teachers who recognise futility). Nevertheless, group work for children can be quite valuable. It helps them to learn ways to interact with each other, how to defuse petty arguments and make headway. Studies carried out by the Institute of Education at University College London showed that when children worked together in groups they behaved adequately and made progress.

However, while many extroverts thrive at the opportunity to interact with large numbers of people and express their ideas, we are executing a method that excludes introverts. What is the aim? Are our education systems trying to mould us into certain kinds of people? American philosopher John Dewey argued that education was not so much about teaching us how to live a practical life but more how to live sensibly in our current situation. Whereas his compatriot George Counts maintained that the purpose of education was more about teaching us to live as members of society. Perhaps education is a mixture of both approaches. Either way, thought needs to be given as to how we find a balance to please every different psychological type. Is it even possible? While group activity may give some the opportunity to flourish, it also, equally, gives many others the opportunity to come crashing down.

Introspection

1. Have you considered the positives and negatives of group work?

2. What group dynamics do you employ?

3. Are you modelling the outcomes of group work in your classroom?

4. Have you reflected on the impact of group work on quieter students?

5. Are you coaching your students in the use of group work?

CHAPTER 6
THE CASE FOR SILENCE

That was it, the final straw. Mrs Screamodo had been officially tipped over the edge. It was period five on a Friday, for goodness' sake. She had well and truly had enough of these children: they were rude, disruptive and downright ignorant. Her voice rose and she shrieked, "Right, that is it! We will be working in silence for the rest of this lesson!"

Instantly adopting their "suitably chastised" facial expressions, the students hunched over their work and the classroom fell quiet. Ten seconds later, low murmuring could be heard in three different pockets of the room. Mrs Screamodo swivelled her head and glared: "I said SILENCE!"

To say it is a shock when I return to the school environment after the serenity of a summer break would be an understatement. In those six weeks, if things have gone according to plan, I have devoured a shelf's worth of books, written lots and spent a great deal of time in silence, all in furtive retreat from my extroverted wife and child.

By the end of the first week back at school, my jangling mind can only be remedied by a long lie-down in a darkened room. In part, this is down to the transition from a stress-free summer to the manic pace of teacher life. More demanding, however, is the sheer loudness of schools. Noise is everywhere: the bell, the lessons, the chat of colleagues, break time, lunchtime…the list goes on.

The overstimulation can be intense. In *The Introvert Advantage: How Quiet People Can Thrive in an Extrovert World*, Marti Olsen Laney writes: "For introverts who have a high level of internal activity, anything coming from the outside raises their intensity level index quickly."

The trouble is, a great deal of the communication among young people is loud. At times they seem to have an almost territorial need to out-shout each other. The teacher Andrew Old (@oldandrewuk) has written about this on his blog:

"Left to their own devices kids get loud, perhaps without realising it. Younger secondary students often just enjoy expending the energy involved in a loud conversation. Older secondary students are often asserting their position in the dominance hierarchy by talking over each other in ever louder voices. Once kids are talking in the classroom, the usual trajectory is for the noise to get louder, unless interrupted, and while sometimes a piece of work that requires an unexpected amount of concentration will cause a class to spontaneously become quieter, that is the memorable exception and not the rule for most classes. In fact, often a class getting quieter without being asked is so exceptional that it is immediately followed by one student shouting 'WHY HAS IT GONE QUIET?'"

Enjoy the silence

In a society that just seems to get louder and more stimulating, the classroom should be – at least some of the time – an environment in which silence is revered. As the previous chapter demonstrated, young people need opportunities for discussion and communication, but they also need to understand why silence is so necessary.

The skills that can be harnessed in silence are undeniably important. The first and most obvious is our ability to concentrate on one thing. Multitasking is the default setting of modern society and this is reflected most clearly in the dwindling attention spans of children. The distractions are much more seductive than in the past: social media and mobile phones are, of course, the most common culprits. Anyone who has run a school trip in the past ten years will know just how much time young people spend on their phones.

Deep thinking can only take place in an environment that enables introspection. Silence, therefore, is a gift and certainly not a punishment. My own ability to think is vastly improved when I work in silence, with minimal distractions. Writing this book, for example, could only take place in solitude early in the morning. Steve Wozniak, co-founder of Apple, has written about the necessity of solitude: "Most inventors and engineers I've met are like me. They're shy and they live in their heads. The very best of them are artists. And artists work best alone … "

When we think of the social dynamics of the classroom, and how quick young people are to acknowledge and respond to their peers, silence seems even more important. It can facilitate a truly productive working environment – not one in which noise is a constant, but one in which thinking is a constant.

Yet, so often in the classroom, silence is stigmatised. In a study published by the *Cambridge Journal of Education*, "Silent Pedagogy and Rethinking Classroom Practice: Structuring Teaching Through Silence Rather Than Talk", Ros Ollin found: "Silence, as an absence of speech, is often problematised in a classroom situation, with the underlying implication that classrooms are for talking – as long as the talking is under the control of the teacher."

Sometimes this "absence of speech" can help to ease anxiety. Endless communication and dialogue can be draining for even the most extroverted students. There is evidence that physical and digital noise negatively affects our focus and sleep, as well as increasing stress hormones and symptoms of anxiety and depression. We have already noted the social pressure that comes into play when dialogue dominates lessons, but it is also important to consider how it can affect thinking and concentration.

Silence is vital to real academic progress and the consolidation of learning. Dave Grimmett (@daveg5478), a head of English, has written about the power of silence on his blog:

"During many observations of teachers over the years, I have commented on a 'productive working environment'. This meant, in essence, that students were behaving, talking about the task (well, those closest to my ear-shot were and they might have been talking cluelessly with a lack of prior knowledge to guide them in the task, but I digress…) and writing stuff down. I may have even replaced 'working' with 'learning' now and again. I'm pretty certain that 90% of the time I would have been wrong to go as far as the 'L' word.

I never cease to be amazed at the way students can cover 2 questions with vague, muddled answers in 30 minutes sometimes in these 'productive working environments', then answer 6 questions sharply in the next 20 minutes of silent work.

It is clear, then, that we have an obligation to create periods of silence in every lesson we teach if we are setting high expectations."

Silence is hard

So why is silence not more celebrated in our classrooms? The first reason is that it can be closely correlated with punishment. Silence is often inflicted on students as the last resort in the behaviour management toolkit. Dr Helen Lees highlights the distinction between useful and imposed silence in her book *Silence in Schools*: "While the former is a deliberate stillness, where pupils are encouraged to sit and reflect, the latter is an enforced quiet, where teachers impose silence."

71

The second reason is that sustaining silence is hard. Anyone who has tried to start a mindfulness habit can appreciate this. Sit in silent contemplation and follow your breath along the path to tranquillity, the advocates say. In reality, controlling our thoughts and impulses is a major challenge.

Yet many of us persist with our mindfulness practice, perhaps because it has been rationalised to us: we have seen the benefits in others, we have read about the research, we understand why it is good for us. But we rarely discuss the importance of silence with our students – we just expect them to adopt it. Arguably, we are not attuned to just how alien silence can feel for young people.

Rationalising silence

If we want young people to embrace silence, we need to make clear why it is so essential. The first few weeks with any new class therefore become extremely important. We want to break the perceived connection between silence and punishment, and instead establish it as a helpful way to enable learning. We want to show students that silent working is in fact about kindness – we are trying to create the best learning environment for them. But silence will be the complete opposite of how many of our students would like to work. They will want to return to their comfort zone: noise.

Silent quotations

We need to think of creative ways to open up conversations about the benefits of silence. It can be useful to start with the image of a mind and ask students to annotate it. What does silence feel like? What are the benefits of silence? How do we achieve it?

A simple lesson starter can be five inspiring quotations that relate to silence. Students have to annotate them, considering what they imply about the power of silence. This can lead to useful discussion about what silence can achieve for us. These are five rather good starting points:

1. "Open your mouth only if what you are going to say is more beautiful than the silence" – *proverb*

2. "The quieter you become, the more you are able to hear" – *Rumi*

3. "A fool is known by his speech; and a wise man by silence' – *Pythagoras*

4. "Only by going alone in silence, without baggage, can one truly get into the heart of the wilderness. All other travel is mere dust and hotels and baggage and chatter" – *John Muir*

5. "Silence is more musical than any song" – *Christina Rossetti*

Employing silence

So, how often should we use silence? And for how long should a class be silent? I would argue that in order to normalise it, a part of every lesson needs to be spent in silent activity. Not only will this help our more introverted students to recharge and refocus their attention, but it will also ensure that all students have the opportunity to think and work independently. Even if it is just for five or 10 minutes, silence will be fruitful in many different ways.

In my own lessons I often refer to this time as "sacred silence" – this helps to give it a status and prestige. Ed Noon (@MrENoon), an English teacher, wrote to me about how he uses silence in his classroom:

"Whenever we read books offering us advice about teaching, we must always remember that the 'classroom tactics' will always be supported or undermined by the culture of the school and the level of meaningful support from those who lead.

One of the key factors in obtaining and maintaining silence in my classroom has been two of the classroom expectations which are supported from the top across my school. 'We listen in silence' and 'We work in silence unless otherwise directed by the teacher'. With the rationale for both clearly explained to both staff and students, everybody understands and appreciates why we strive for silence.

How do I sustain working in silence? At the beginning of every lesson, as the students complete their arrival task (nearly always a short knowledge quiz), any interruption or noise is met with a reminder from me that it is unkind to interrupt somebody else while they are trying to retrieve nearly forgotten information from their mind. One of our key attitudes is kindness, so by focusing on breaking the silence as being unkind, students feel they understand that silence is not just for their own learning, but that they have a duty to support their peers as well.

When students are about to begin a period of time working in silence, I remind them that this is their opportunity to show off, a chance to 'show what you know'. I share my expectation that their work will be impressive, and I remind them that excellence is only possible when their mind is fully focused on recalling and implementing the best of what they have thought and learnt during the teaching which has culminated in this piece of work.

For me, it is essential the case for silence is aligned with a great overemphasis on warmth. We do not seek silence because we are cruel; we seek silence because we are kind, because we love our students, and because we believe they can think and learn just as well as anyone else. Following a piece of silent study, warm praise for the whole group is essential and so is communicating how proud we are of their efforts. As students leave my classroom, I hold the door open and thank each individually with a smile for their work during my lesson.

Of course, we also have reactive measures to ensure those who are unkind by breaking the silence are not permitted to do so repeatedly. Breaking the silence receives a warning on the board. Nothing else happens and the reason for the warning is calmly narrated by me, the teacher. If a student is warned a second time, they will take 20 minutes of extended reflection time after school to think about how they will be kinder next time, but they stay in the lesson. If the same student interrupts the lesson for a third time, they are kindly asked to leave to go to a room known in my school as the reset room. Here, a member of staff will support the student in reflecting upon the expectations they didn't meet this time round and prepare them to return to their next timetabled lesson; they have reset their mind and are ready to start again.

How do I make sure silence is meaningful? It would be foolish to take a silent room as a proxy for hard work and learning. There is nothing to stop a student from apathetically sitting in silence while every person around them works hard in silence. However, having a silent classroom makes it much easier to survey the room and identify who needs support.

During the first couple of years of my teaching career, I darted here, there and everywhere around my classroom in response to the siren call of those who sought attention. These were not the students who needed the most help. In a disaster situation, attend to those who are silent before you attend to those who are crying out for help.

Now, I am able to stand at the side, the back, or front of my room and watch my students work. I can spot a student not working in an instant and quickly visit them to judge whether it is a case of 'can't' or 'won't'. When all are happily working, I now also have the headspace to think carefully who to select to mark their work over their shoulder and whisper feedback, praise or encouragement in their ear. This doesn't happen too much to avoid over-narrating, but just enough to show the class I am watching and I am looking. A tick over the shoulder, a 'good' or 'keep going' is enough to show my care. Finally, it allows me to formally assess work in the lesson (meaning no marking outside the lesson) and it allows me to catch misconceptions or errors while they are hot and address them right away."

This is packed full of humane and helpful guidance on how to build a culture in which silence is valued by both teachers and students. Here are some other ways to help sustain silence in class:

- **Use a timer.** This supports students' metacognitive abilities, as they can track how effectively they are completing the task against the timer. It allows them to work at their own pace without distraction. And they always know how much longer they need to be silent for.

- **Quiet behaviour management.** Rather than breaking the concentration of the majority by loudly berating the minority who are not working or thinking in silence, adopt the quiet behavioural strategies we will unpick later in this book. Express genuine horror when individuals break the code of silence – this will help to preserve it.

- **Silent starters.** Sometimes the transition to a new task or a new lesson can prove troublesome. A silent starter can signal that a change in thinking is required – this routine can save energy for students and also for teachers. Indeed, creating more opportunities for silence in lessons allows teachers to think with more clarity and therefore make a better explanation, ask a better question and teach a better lesson.

Over-narration

Such techniques are useful, but unless we curb our own impulse to speak, silent conditions will not be possible. One of my worst habits in the classroom is elaborately over-narrating just about every aspect of learning. Even during periods of silent work I am prone to loud interjections of "You are doing really well, really good levels of focus here" or "You have three minutes remaining!", thus breaking the silence and the concentration.

We must learn to curb ourselves as well as our students. Think carefully before you break the silence – will your injection help them to sustain their focus? Before I speak, I now ask myself: how will this support the learning in the room?

Moments of complete silence while we model a skill can also have a real impact on learning. Neil Almond (@Mr_AlmondED), a primary teacher in London, told me how he employs this in his own classroom:

> "Our working memory is a mysterious thing. Cognitive science can now tell us that our working memory is not one single entity but rather is made up of two different components: the phonological loop and the visuospatial sketchpad. Simply put, the phonological loop processes the sounds, while the visuospatial sketchpad processes the visual stimuli. Teachers can use

the knowledge of both these channels to present information in two ways – auditory and visual. If talking about the countries in the continent of Europe, it would make sense to present this information through talk while simultaneously having a map of Europe projected for the class.

What the phonological loop also processes is our 'inside voice'. The voice that you are reading these very words in. It is here that we have a slight problem. When we model a task – say, how to use long multiplication, so solving 652 x 28 – and provide an explanation at the same time, the phonological loop risks being overwhelmed as it tries to process the teacher's explanation as well as the internal thoughts of the student – the 'Why did he put that number there?' and 'I am not sure what 6 x 8 is'.

This can cause cognitive overload of the working memory and, as a result, prevent the new information being presented from going into long-term memory. To put it another way, when you are reading something with your 'inside voice' you cannot actually process what another person may be telling you in conversation. To that end, silence is a teacher's best tool. But not student silence – the teacher being silent.

Often known as Silent Teacher, and a staple of my teaching since developing my understanding of working memory, this describes a technique where a teacher models a process by writing an example on the board, but without talking while this modelling is happening. Once the example has been completed, the teacher then gives the explanation of the 'what' and the 'why'. The benefits of modelling in silence are two-fold. It allows the students' phonological loop to initially focus on those internal questions that they have about the process; then we can focus the student's working memory on our verbal explanation, helping to manage the cognitive load placed on the phonological loop in the working memory. The other benefit to this approach is that when you begin the modelling process in silence, the students are also completely silent.

When modelling in silence, it is often helpful to consider those internal questions the students may have and draw their attention to certain parts of your modelling that you really want them to think about. Say, on the board, you present Year 4 students with:

$$652$$
$$\text{x } 28$$

To help them understand the process more, you could tap the 2, 8 and x with your pen to draw attention to the fact that you will be multiplying these digits first. This is useful in order to get them thinking about what you want during the modelling process without talking yourself."

So, that's the end of Part I of this book. The strategies we have examined will hopefully go some way towards helping our more introverted students – and indeed all our students – to thrive in the classroom. But what about our more introverted colleagues? What can we learn from quieter teachers? And what might applying a quiet lens to our work in schools help us to achieve? We will consider this in Part II.

A quiet reflection

Mary Myatt (@MaryMyatt) is an education adviser whose books include Hopeful Schools: Building Humane Communities *and* The Curriculum: Gallimaufry to Coherence.

Quiet is the jewel in the crown of learning and I make the case on three counts.

First, in order to process new information, gain insights into knotty problems and develop new ideas, we need stillness and quiet as a counterpoint to talk.

Second, our words are important – they are an expression of thoughts, insights and nuance – but they need time to be processed and this requires quiet.

Third, I have often used quiet in classrooms. Not as an oppressive mechanism for cutting down chatter, but as a way of creating a space for students to go deeper. Because I believe that silence is important, I would get my students to practise being silent. Just doing nothing but being with their thoughts. We would practise this initially for one minute, and I would warn them that it is difficult and that some of them would struggle, and some might even giggle. And that this is OK until we get the hang of it. The surprising thing I found was that after a few goes, when the giggles had gone (letting them know this might happen made it less likely and resulted in peer pressure to maintain the silence), students welcomed this. They knew that it created a space for them to process ideas, before we opened the material up for discussion. They knew that it made a difference.

Introspection

1. In your classroom, is silence celebratory or related to punishment?

2. How often do you share the reasons for silence?

3. Do you build a silent section into every lesson to enable genuine thinking and independent practice?

4. Are you prone to over-narrating what happens in your lessons?

5. Have you tried the Silent Teacher technique?

PART II
QUIET FOR TEACHERS
AND LEADERS

Quiet people have the loudest minds
Stephen Hawking

CHAPTER 7
THE QUIET ENVIRONMENT

Solitude matters, and for some people,
it's the air they breathe
Susan Cain

Last year I worked four days a week, in order to spend each Friday looking after my (extremely well-named) little boy. It was wonderful and I loved having that time with him, but there was one problem: it meant I didn't have my own classroom. Instead, I taught in almost 20 different classrooms in every two-week timetable.

A few weeks into this nomadic existence, I couldn't work out why I was so stressed out and wired. I was an experienced teacher, so why was I back to waking up early and finding everything so overwhelming? Why did I feel like I was rushing around on autopilot?

Ironically, I had released my first book, *Slow Teaching*, six months previously. Its subtitle, "On finding calm, clarity and impact in the classroom", haunted me. My slump seemed extreme: I was shattered by the end of the day and my anxiety levels had rocketed.

On reflection, it wasn't particularly surprising: introverts such as me are easily overstimulated by loud workplaces. According to Dr Laurie Helgoe, the author of *Introvert Power: Why Your Inner Life is Your Hidden Strength*, "Introverts need quieter environments, lower or more focused lighting, and plenty of personal space." Sprinting across a comprehensive school of 2500 students to find my next classroom was hardly conducive to a zen state of mind.

Although the year did improve, and I regained a little calm, the experience reminded me of just how important our professional environments are. So what can all teachers, not just those with a need for solitude, do to find a balance between calm and energy in their environment? When we consider how much performance and adrenaline are associated with teaching, this question becomes even more urgent.

When he was running Microsoft, Bill Gates would isolate himself in a cabin in the woods for a "think week" twice a year. We may not all be able to emulate Gates, but we can certainly make practical changes to our work habits to allow ourselves time for quiet. Just like Gates, who came up with the idea to launch Internet Explorer during a think week, a bit of space for thought might make a real difference to our work.

Classroom design

First, let's explore how teachers might be able to apply a quiet focus in their classroom environment. In *Slow Teaching*, I wrote a chapter called "The minimalistic classroom". What I didn't realise at the time was that this was basically a manifesto for the ideal introvert setting. I argued that although the temptation is to cover every classroom wall with visual stimuli, this is actually counterintuitive. Not only can it divert students' attention, but it can also distract and wear out teachers.

I suggested that an environment of clear, organised simplicity could help to keep students and teachers calm and focused. Tranquil classrooms can be refuges from the relentlessness of the wider school environment. There is a need for what TS Eliot describes as "the still point of the turning world", and if we can't find that in our classrooms, we will struggle.

Restorative niches

Knowing when to take a moment of quiet for ourselves can also have a transformative impact on our wellbeing. We often read stories of "selfless" teachers who make themselves available at all hours of the day and cram in their lunch while hosting yet another intervention session with their GCSE classes. After school they spend more time with students like Lucy and Devon, who just can't seem to grasp equations. Their evenings are similarly packed full of work and their holidays function merely as recovery time from the intensity of term.

Of course, long hours contribute to the exhaustion these teachers will inevitably experience, but it is exacerbated by the endless communication and interaction. The school day places significant interpersonal demands on teachers and the reality is that we rarely get any downtime. If morning lessons are followed by breaks and lunchtimes that are spent with others, and then meetings or phone calls at the end of the day, teachers are denied any chance to recharge their batteries. For those more inclined to quiet, this can be a sure step towards burnout.

Teachers need to embrace a degree of healthy selfishness and find some restorative niches. The amount of downtime required depends on the individual, but discovering what works for you is vital. We need to define our social and interpersonal boundaries, and enforce them. Take some comfort from the words of Lord Byron: "I only go out to get me a fresh appetite for being alone."

We all need time to decompress, no matter if we are extroverted or introverted. "I tell introverts to stop bragging that they missed lunch or don't get any breaks," Helgoe has said. "All they are telling me is that they are not feeding themselves mentally and creatively, and this will show itself in compromised work products and services." Being overwhelmed and overloaded is not going to help us provide the best for our students. In my nomadic journeying across the school, I had no time to pause and recharge.

Building downtime into the school day is challenging, but it is possible. It can be as simple as taking some time for yourself at break and lunchtime. I asked teachers to share their strategies for finding downtime in the school day. Some work in environments that facilitate and encourage restorative moments – one teacher in a Catholic school, for example, told me they often sought refuge in the school chapel. Others have a designated space for reading in their classroom, which can be a haven for quieter students during lessons and for teachers during breaks. One teacher admitted taking refuge in the isolation room, conventionally used to manage challenging behaviour, confessing that it was "surprisingly relaxing!" And an unexpected number of people said they shut themselves away in their car for five minutes.

The Cambridge professor Brian Little, the author of *Me, Myself and Us: The Science of Personality and the Art of Well-being*, offers another surprising place of sanctuary: the toilet. As Susan Cain wrote in her book *Quiet*, "I sometimes go to the bathroom to escape the slings and arrows of outrageous extroverts."

During her teaching years, my mother would take a lunchtime walk. We don't all have the beauty of the Highlands of Scotland on our doorstep, but spending a few moments in nature can be restorative. If this isn't possible, the school library can be a brilliant retreat for quieter and more reflective students, as well as their teachers.

Quieter people are not hermits who have no desire to connect with others, but we have to claim some part of our day for ourselves – and not just our working day. Teaching is a job that can eat into evenings and weekends, but it must not be allowed to dominate our lives. Being clear on our working patterns and defining how we want to work (rather than letting teaching define how we work) have to be priorities in order to achieve work-life balance.

Evenings should be an opportunity to detach from the mentally overwhelming world of school. Setting a time when you stop working, regardless of what still needs to be done, will allow you to switch off from the professional world and help to ensure a restful night's sleep. There must also be a cut-off point for email and social media. As we shall see later, social media can be an inspiring learning environment for teachers, but it never stops – it is perpetual dialogue. Sometimes it is more healthy to step away and think about something else. The more we associate our identity with our professional selves, the less able we are to leave stress and anxiety behind.

Be open

In preparation for this book, I spoke to many introverted teachers who were concerned about how their colleagues perceived them. One teacher, who asked to remain anonymous, sent me the following: "During my training I struggled to have a presence, but that changed during my RQT year. I notice that by the time I get home I am very introverted, as I need my space to recharge for the next day. When it comes to pupils, I would say I am slightly extroverted, but my introverted side comes out a lot with other staff. This is my fourth year teaching and it's only this year I have started to interact more with other staff and go to the staffroom more. I never did previously. I have struggled to make meaningful relationships beyond work with other staff, due to being introverted."

Many quieter teachers may recognise this experience: their dynamism can be sapped by students and therefore they struggle to invest energy in relationships with colleagues. This is something I have wrestled with: how do we show people that we are not antisocial, or even reserved? How can we be open about our personality type and how we function best?

I would argue, however, that at times quieter individuals can be their own worst enemy. In reality, most people are genuinely understanding of personality differences. More often it is our own inner dialogue that is negative and fretful. We might use that inner voice to criticise ourselves and bemoan our need for quiet, rather than treating ourselves with the compassion we would show others.

I personally find this most problematic in group situations, in which I usually contribute very little. Instead, my mind is turning certain questions over and over. How do these extroverts have such boundless energy and charisma? How are they so gregarious all the time? When everyone else appears so outgoing and confident, it can be challenging to maintain your equilibrium.

So, how can we make school life more manageable? First, we have to accept that we are not the same as our extroverted colleagues – we need time in solitude or quiet. This is not an active choice: the reality is that our innate natures demand it.

The more open we are with those around us, the better. It is important to explain that we need space to decompress, and this can be done with good humour: "I just have to escape for a few minutes and recharge" can answer why we are in our rooms after a challenging morning. Being open with colleagues about these individual preferences can help to form positive relationships. And there is real value in sharing these preferences with students: it can normalise emotions that a number of them may be feeling.

We have seen that our professional environment has an impact on how we feel psychologically, as does our capacity to find moments of solace and solitude. Yet, for quieter, more sensitive individuals working in education, there is a more serious threat. In the next chapter we will turn our attention to the issue of burnout.

A quiet reflection

Dan Rodriguez-Clark (@interactmaths) is a maths teacher and a teaching and learning coordinator at Markham College in Lima, Peru. He runs the website interactive-maths.com

Over the last year or so, I have become much more aware of – and comfortable with – the fact that I am an introvert. Much of this change came with reading the excellent *Quiet* by Susan Cain, which opened my eyes to the fact that introversion is widespread and, although Western society has an "extrovert ideal", introverts have a quiet power to get things done.

One of the biggest realisations for me was that introverts and extroverts react differently to stimulation: introverts are very easily overstimulated and they are detail-focused. This rang true with all my own experiences. When chatting with a group of people, perhaps in the staffroom, I find it difficult when more than one conversation is going on within close proximity. I become overstimulated, finding myself half-listening to each conversation and unable to fully participate in any. I also become fixated on the details of what we talk about, rather than the big picture, preferring to talk about something in-depth rather than chit-chat. I often end up sitting quietly as a bystander to the conversation, sometimes feeling a little awkward.

Another key realisation was that introverts need time to decompress after being with others. It is not that introverts do not like to socialise, but rather that the huge amount of stimulation that occurs within a large social group is draining for an introvert. They need time to get away from this and be inside their own heads. Whereas extroverts live outside themselves, thinking things through by discussing ideas, introverts live within their own heads, preferring to engage in deep thought. Introverts are, by their very nature, quiet.

With these ideas in mind, my classroom is my haven at work. I am fortunate to have my own classroom that is rarely used by other teachers (I am kicked out for one hour a week this year). Some days I eat lunch by myself in my classroom, taking the time to enjoy a little quiet "me time". Other days I go to the staffroom to socialise. Most of my free periods are spent alone in my room planning. This is the work that thrills me the most: engaging in deep thought about the content I am to teach, the order I want to teach it in, and how to explain the ideas clearly. I find I am more productive at this when working alone, and my classroom is where I do this.

Which brings me to my classroom...

Early in my career, I was known for my displays. I would trawl the internet to find great ideas, spend hours printing and laminating, and even had things like a puzzle corner where I would change the puzzles each week. But my thoughts on this have changed dramatically over the last two years.

My classroom is now much more minimalist. I have clearly labelled shelves at the back where classes leave their books, scrap paper can be found and mini whiteboards are stored. The walls are relatively bare. My desk area is the only space with a bit more to it: there are some family photos and notes to myself on the wall.

When thinking about displays, I now live by two mantras:

1.   Will I refer to the display in my teaching?

2.   Can students read the display from their seats?

Whereas my walls used to be covered with displays, both on boards and stuck to the walls themselves, I now have limited posters and those I do have serve a very specific purpose. I currently have two displays. The first is a series of four quotes/ideas from cognitive science that I have around the top of the walls. These are:

- "Memory is the residue of thought" – *Daniel T Willingham*

- "Practice makes permanent" – *Anders Ericsson*

- "Learning occurs over a long time" – *Hermann Ebbinghaus*

- "Our working memories are limited" – *John Sweller*

They are printed big enough to be read from anywhere in the room, and I often refer to them when talking about studying and learning with my classes.

The second display is linked to an initiative we have in our department called The Approaches to Learning Mathematics. This includes skills such as perseverance, mathematical communication and resourcefulness, with descriptors as to what each looks like in my subject. I started with having the poster displayed, but this fails my second mantra, so I have replaced it with just the titles, and students have a copy of the full thing stuck in their books. This way I can refer to the idea in passing in class, but refer to details too if needed.

I do not have displays of excellent work either, as these are usually not visible to students and rarely looked at. I use a visualiser in my teaching for modelling and I also use this to show good work. If I see an excellent piece of work as I observe students working, I will put it under the visualiser and discuss with students why it is good. This is Doug Lemov's idea of "show call" and it stops the walls becoming cluttered with pieces of work.

With few displays, I have had all the display boards in my room replaced with extra whiteboards. I now have three big whiteboards on three of the four walls, giving me nine large working spaces. I use these with students regularly, getting them up to work on the boards in pairs, or for teaching smaller groups. This allows me to easily see their work and, as students can easily erase at any point, opens them up to trying new things.

Why have I made such a dramatic change to my classroom? There are two things that have fed into this decision. The more compelling argument for me was to consider the introverts in my class. If, as I have discussed above, introverts are easily overstimulated, then having large displays could lead to an environment that is a little uncomfortable for those introverts. Or maybe it just wears them down being so stimulated. I would rather give them (and myself) a space where they can focus on what I want them to learn in a particular lesson.

The other was my reading of ideas from cognitive science, and in particular the redundancy effect from cognitive load theory (see the 2017 literature review *Cognitive Load Theory: Research That Teachers Really Need to Understand*, published by the Centre for Education Statistics and Evaluation in Australia). This suggests that if there are items in our environment that are not relevant to what we are currently trying to learn, then we will have to use mental capacity to filter them out, reducing the capacity we have for learning. This is something that benefits both introverts and extroverts. By creating a "quiet" space (in both auditory and visual volume) I am hoping to help all students settle into a working frame of mind where they can truly focus on the task and learning at hand.

Schools are largely designed for the extrovert. We spend our days working in groups, presenting to others, sitting in noisy cafeterias, with friends at break time, and in classrooms which are often covered in displays and require us to discuss, share and collaborate with groups of up to 30 people. For the introvert, these are all tiring experiences – both the students and the teachers. So, if I can provide a little bit of quiet for the students for five lessons a week, then I think that is important.

Introspection

1. Is your classroom an environment in which you feel calm and relaxed?

2. Would your classroom benefit from a minimalist cleanse?

3. Are you making space for yourself during the school day?

4. Could you employ any of the restorative niches mentioned in this chapter?

5. Are you being open with your colleagues about your personality preferences?

CHAPTER 8
AVOIDING BURNOUT

*Take a rest. A field that is rested
gives a beautiful crop*
Ovid

A short journey through the etymology of the adjective "quiet" proves interesting in the context of burnout in teaching. It stems from the Latin *quietus*, meaning to be calm, at rest and free from exertion, and is borrowed from the Anglo-French and Middle French *quiete*, first appearing in the 14th century. For a modern teacher, deep into the demands of a term, is there a time when we feel truly free from exertion? Do the words "calm" and "at rest" spring to mind when we consider our day with young people? Exertion and teaching are interconnected. Quiet and teaching, unfortunately, do not have such a strong relationship.

Stress affects us all in different ways and everyone, of course, is at risk of exhaustion. People with quieter, more introverted dispositions, as we shall see, can be even more susceptible to burnout. Being self-aware and taking the necessary steps to protect your mental health are essential for longevity and happiness in the teaching profession. Importantly, these are also vital for our capacity to teach well. We cannot do our jobs properly when we are stressed, overworked and exhausted.

What causes burnout?

Burnout was first explored in a scientific paper by the psychologist Herbert Freudenberger in 1974. He described it as a series of symptoms relating to work's excessive demands. Ultimately, burnout is a state of emotional, physical and mental exhaustion caused by excessive and prolonged stress. It occurs when you feel overwhelmed, emotionally drained and unable to meet the constant demands placed on you.

Burnout has become one of the most widely discussed mental health problems in our society. Its prevalence in education in the UK and elsewhere is worryingly high. The reasons for this are complex and varied, but more awareness of what may be contributing to the frequency of burnout can be useful for all who are involved in education.

Student behaviour

As we shall see later, in a specific chapter on this issue, poor behaviour has the ability to send the stress hormone, cortisol, sky high in teachers. Frequent confrontation and challenge can leave teachers feeling dispirited, stressed and anxious. Stress, of course, is an evolutionary response to danger in which our fight or flight instinct is activated. Hostile and challenging classroom environments inevitably have a significant impact on our stress levels – we can feel the fight or flight instinct far too often.

We have all experienced these emotions, but burnout can occur when behaviour doesn't improve, leading to sleepless nights and extreme stress over a long period of time. When this is combined with limited support from management, it can become even more isolating.

Heavy workload

The risk of burnout rises when there is a lack of work-life balance and when teachers work at an unsustainable rate. The intensity of term time can result in a lack of sleep and long hours, with respite found only in the school holidays.

The fact is that teaching is a job we can never really press pause on. Teachers, who can be among society's most idealistic and conscientious people, often feel the need to work harder than is healthy. Such feelings can be heightened by the individuals in the staffroom who talk loudly of how many hours they have worked that week and how their weekend will be stolen by yet more marking. Effort often replaces efficiency in the teaching profession. We need to change the conversation so it is about the impact of these hours on young people.

School culture and managerial policies can be hugely influential in the wellbeing of staff. I worked at a school in which the headteacher arrived before 6am and left well into the evening. This sent the message to staff that this was an environment in which long hours took precedence over anything else, including productivity.

Teachers are the masters of the holiday countdown: "Only 15 days to go!" This is not because we don't enjoy our jobs, but rather that the holidays can be our only chance to catch our breath. What we need is the capacity to rest and recover not only during holidays, but also during our working weeks. Freya Odell (@fod3), an English teacher, wrote to me about how she often feels overwhelmed by the interpersonal demands of teaching and how she prioritises quiet to ensure her own wellbeing:

> "The term 'introvert' has been a revolution in understanding myself. While I am happy and confident in the classroom, I really struggle with adults on a larger scale. I hate being surrounded by large groups and find the space quite intimidating. I also hate being surrounded by people I don't know. I hate public speaking but have tried to conquer that beast. People see me and see someone who is confident. They can't believe that I am practically phobic about it when I present, but I am, and I have cried and been sick ahead of speaking to a large group of people.
>
> I value quiet above all else. I think this is because it restores my energy. The staffroom is quite a sociable place, so I tend to go to the library to work instead, where I know it is quiet and I can get my work done. If I am tired, I sometimes find it hard to socialise even with my friends and need some distance...this is especially evident at the end of a term. Sometimes it can come across to people as standoffish, but really I am just protecting myself."

Introversion and burnout

I burnt out spectacularly in my late twenties. I had taken on far too much responsibility far too soon as an assistant headteacher; this, combined with working ludicrous hours and obsessively running more than 50 miles a week, led to my becoming seriously ill.

I went from being fitter and healthier than I had ever been (I had never had a day off) to being off work for almost two months. For a time I couldn't even get out of bed and the experience was terrifying. I was physically and emotionally depleted. I didn't think I would ever get back to how I had felt before, physically or mentally.

The mental struggle was far more challenging than the physical one and for about a year afterwards I was a functioning insomniac. I felt utterly demotivated and depressed. It was a stark and humbling reminder of just how fragile our mental health is – nobody is invincible. The pressure we can feel in teaching to be a martyr to the cause, and to place all other concerns above our own, is neither healthy nor sustainable.

Today, I am passionate about prioritising care for oneself and others. We often invest a significant amount of time and effort in how we present to the world on the outside, but nurturing ourselves on the inside – our psychological wellbeing – is equally, if not more, important.

Forget perfectionism

There is one common trait of introversion that all quieter teachers will be familiar with: we are prone to extreme overthinking and overanalysing. We have already noted the positives of introversion: self-motivation, the ability to concentrate deeply and a desire to get things right. But that last trait can sometimes veer into perfectionism.

Being aware of this internal voice and its demand for perfection is the first step towards finding balance. Having a designated cut-off time in the evenings or at weekends, after which all work is put away, is one of the best ways to tackle the inner voice. Unfortunately, teaching can be a job in which you never really feel on top of things: there is always more you can do. But we need to learn to recognise when we are no longer able to work and concentrate effectively. Anything we do after this time will just serve to build stress and anxiety, leaving us more susceptible to burnout.

Find a mentor

We all need somebody at work who we can open up to, someone who will help us to gain clarity over that internal wrangling. Quieter individuals are unlikely to share their frustrations and concerns with a full staffroom, so the temptation is to bottle them up. But this can cause stress and resentment.

Quieter characters often prioritise meaningful conversations, which is why mentoring can be an extremely useful process for them. In my first school I had an absolutely terrific mentor; she walked me, emotionally and practically, through my first four years of teaching. She was the greatest listener I have ever come across and had a wisdom gained from a long and successful career in education.

We all need advice and support at times, and mentoring means we have a designated person to turn to. Talking things through with them can restore calm and motivation, and they can help to design that all important defence against burnout: a strategic plan for how we are going to use our time.

Asking someone to mentor you might be challenging for introverted teachers, but the rewards are significant. For those who cry that there is never the time, the reality is that any time invested in mentoring conversations will make us more productive and improve the teaching that takes place in the classroom.

Social media

Social media can be a superb resource for teachers: a wealth of information and guidance is available at the click of a button. It can inspire, challenge and allow for collaboration on a scale that has not been seen before. The insight into what other teachers are doing in their classrooms is what I find so useful, rather than the tenuous and ego-driven debates about every aspect of education.

For more introverted teachers, social media is invaluable. It can be a safe place to converse with the teaching community, free from eye contact, noise and the pressure to come up with an immediate response. Yet, for all the benefits of social media, it can fuel the workaholic and perfectionist in us. People can use it as a platform to present a too-perfect version of themselves and what happens in their classrooms. And, in a profession in which time is short, social media can steal precious hours from us. It can lead to a procrastination habit that ends up making us more, not less, stressed.

A social media break can be a very positive way to sustain your energy and passion for teaching. Just one social-media-free day a week can help, but a more sustained break can be even more beneficial. I take two months off social media every year and find this a time of real clarity and focus. Such a long break may not be necessary for everyone, but just being reflective about how we use social media and how it makes us feel can be productive and lead to long-term changes in habits.

Email can also be a real issue for teachers. I moved from a school that had an almost blanket ban on emailing to one in which emails seemed to fly in at a rate of 100 an hour. Of course, perfectionist me tried desperately to keep up, in order to make sure I didn't miss anything important, but this just sent my stress levels soaring. I have also spoken to teachers who receive emails from parents late into the evening, enquiring about homework and other matters.

I think we should be able to leave our emails behind when we exit the school gates. It should be part of the process of closing off the working day and preparing for a restful evening. Sending or replying to emails late into the evening certainly shouldn't be seen as a badge of honour.

Regular exercise

Exercise can restore the energy that is depleted by a long day of interaction in school. Even a short walk can have a positive impact, bringing some much-needed peace and stillness. It facilitates a switch from high stimulation back down to low stimulation.

This quiet, solitary time is often what we need to gain perspective and leave behind the classroom. Nelson Mandela, a self-described introvert, had a particularly intense exercise regime. On Robben Island, he would get up at 5am to run for an hour around his cell. "I enjoyed the discipline and solitariness of long-distance running, which allowed me to escape from the hurly-burly of everyday life," he reflected.

We might not match Mandela's discipline, but no matter how bad we are feeling, any form of exercise can help to restore a positive frame of mind, even if it is just getting off the bus a stop early.

Gratitude

Stress can lead to tunnel vision that blinds us to the wonderful things that may be happening all around us. Sometimes we need to allow ourselves time to pause and consider what has stood out, resonated and moved us. Writing down three good things that have taken place each day can be immensely powerful, helping to break cycles of negative thinking. We can then start to share this gratitude with others, paying more compliments and generally being more positive to be around.

A diary or journal habit is a useful way to work through feeling and thought patterns that might be preventing us from presenting the best version of ourselves. When I was at my lowest after I burnt out, I started to write in a diary every night. Just ten minutes of writing helped to make sense of my feelings of failure, and seeing my thoughts written down often gave me a better sense of perspective. There is no need to moderate what you write: it is entirely personal and private, so be as searingly honest as you need to be.

Mindful teachers

Perhaps the most obvious and useful of all solitary activities is meditation. The misconception persists that meditation requires incense and tantra-style music in order to be effective, but fundamentally it just involves sitting in silence for a period of time and concentrating on your breathing.

Meditation is not for everyone, but it has proved extremely helpful for me. For introverts and quieter individuals, the mind-body stillness may well come more easily – after all, we are already expert in all things reflective and internal. I try to give at least ten minutes a day to my own meditation habit. I don't manage it every day, but it is something that I always come back to. It requires motivation and often I have to drag myself out of bed earlier than I might want, yet the benefits are significant. It also can appear counterintuitive: when you feel extremely busy, how can you possibly prioritise sitting and doing nothing? But when you return to your work, it is with increased focus and energy.

Just ask Yuval Noah Harari, the author of the best-selling *Sapiens: A Brief History of Humankind*, who goes on 60-day silent retreats and meditates for two hours a day. This is what he has said about his meditation habit: "First of all, it's the ability to focus. When you train the mind to focus on something like the breath, it also gives you the discipline to focus on much bigger things and to really tell the difference between what's important and everything else."

The benefits of mindfulness can be shared with others in the school environment. The teacher Philip Anderson (@dukkhaboy), whose meditation habit is deeply connected with his work, has had a real impact on his colleagues and young people:

"My meditation practice and my teacher training started in the same year; I have never done one without the other. A few years ago, they became more closely linked, and not only do I have a daily meditation practice that affects my teaching, but I also teach timetabled mindfulness lessons to teenagers and a mindfulness-based stress reduction (MBSR) course to staff.

My own practice has always influenced the attitude I try to bring to my teaching. Mindfulness gives me a context within which all parts of my job can fit. No matter how awful the day, or the year, or the pressure, or the exhaustion, there is an option to be aware of the wider context of each situation. No matter how excellent the lesson, or the moment, or the pupils' learning, mindfulness means there is more chance of noticing the experience and being grateful for it.

The space mindfulness can create allows the opportunity for a broader, more honest and accurate awareness to arise. So whatever the situation – good or bad, stressful or easy – a moment of mindfulness brought on by regular long-term practice of meditation can make you happier, more grateful, or at least less upset. Subsequently, this wisdom will allow more compassion and kindness to arise for yourself and those around you.

In the last five years I have started to teach mindfulness to pupils within our school curriculum and in the last two years to groups of staff within the academy trust. Teaching mindfulness in the classroom is a fundamentally different way of working. I am offering my pupils an experience and an approach to day-to-day life that they can try. I set 'home practice', not homework, which of course is impossible to take in and mark anyhow. But if it doesn't work for them, no bother – as long as they have given it a go.

There is no doubt that the mindfulness course I teach is having an impact on the pupils. Each year between 65% and 75% of pupils have said that they are likely or very likely to use mindfulness in the future. This year, when I have started to ask students to write down an example of when they have used mindfulness, the responses were fabulous. The responses ranged from the immense – 'When my granddad was ill in hospital I used mindfulness and became more OK with my sadness' – to the mundane – 'I was worried about my science test but after I did some finger breathing I just got on with it'.

In the MBSR courses I have run for staff, the reactions have been equally positive. But I am always wary of claiming a measurable impact from mindfulness. I do not want people to come to mindfulness or meditation wanting to achieve a goal. In *A Monk's Guide to Happiness: Meditation in the 21st Century*, Gelong Thubten writes: 'If we are meditating for wellbeing, we are telling ourselves we don't have that wellbeing; and so we perpetuate a state of deficiency.'

Instead, I believe that mindfulness and meditation are providing children and adults with the opportunity to be happier in their lives and kinder to those around them and also to themselves."

We are, as the poet William Ernest Henley would have it, the captains of our own souls, but often what happens in the school environment lies out of our control. We have to find what makes us feel calmer and better about our life and our work, and what works for one teacher may appear utterly ludicrous to another. Then, once we have found our own strategy, we must be disciplined and prioritise it, even in the face of seemingly endless to-do lists.

A quiet reflection

Tom Rees (@TomRees_77) is the executive director of school leadership at Ambition Institute. This is an extract from his book Wholesome Leadership.

It was about 18 months into my first headship when my body finally said: "Enough is enough." It came about a month after an Ofsted inspection – one that had been long awaited and had been the focus of our work pretty much since I started at the school. It was successful, but the process was gruelling.

I was a young head, desperate to prove myself through the challenges which had come thick and fast, including tackling underperformance, parental challenges and the pressures of trying to secure a good Ofsted judgement in a village school where the expectations were high. Every school has its challenges and, while I would be the first to acknowledge the difficult work that goes on in more deprived communities, the raised expectations and sometimes vigorous parental engagement that come with working in a more affluent community bring about their own pressures.

Looking back, it was pretty obvious that I was heading for a fall. The hours and intensity just weren't sustainable, yet I was so determined to succeed and for the school to do well that I just kept adding everything to my job list and saying yes. There were lots of bad habits that I'd fallen into; it is not difficult to see why I got to the point of burnout, particularly while trying to juggle the demands of a young family at the same time.

Does any of this sound familiar?

- **Unsustainable working hours**. I was so determined to be able to cope with everything on my plate that I started getting up earlier in the morning and finishing later each night. I was setting my alarm clock for 5am in order to try to get some work done before the family woke up. I would get to school early, stay late and then typically work at home in the evening until 11pm or midnight several nights a week.

- **Broken sleep**. I was so wired when I went to bed, I found it difficult to get to sleep. As I tried to sleep, I would often remember several other things that I needed to do. I would lie and think these over; I would be making notes on my phone for the morning; and I would get back up and go and do them.

- **Weekend working**. As a teacher, I had often worked on Sunday afternoons or evenings. This had now become so regular, it almost felt a part of my core hours. I would find myself spending parts of Sunday looking forward to the point when I could switch on my laptop and work.

- **Constant email**. These were the early days of primary school email and smartphones, and the lure of having access to email on the go was too much. I was continually online and accessible, with notifications pinging constantly, and fell into the trap of replying too quickly to everything that came in.

- **Rehearsing hypothetical conversations**. I developed a habit of practising future difficult conversations in the car wherever I went. I could be driving to work and I'd be talking out loud to an imaginary Ofsted inspector, arguing the toss about something to do with Year 3 data trends. Or I'd be in the shower having it out with a parent in anticipation of a meeting that might never happen. This was one of the most unhelpful habits, looking back.

Exhaustion, anxiety and panic attacks were the price I paid: debilitating and terrifying moments that would creep in and get me at any time of the day or night. It was a difficult period and I still have a note that I wrote describing my symptoms from that time, which reads as follows:

- Not myself.

- Tired.

- Feel like I'm living in a bubble.

- Can't face things or cope.

- Want to stay in bed.

- Stomach and chest pains.

- Short of breath.

- Nothing's real.

- Want to switch off.

- No emotions/unsociable.

- Anxious.

I keep this as a reminder of how bad things got, and a prompt to keep a healthier balance and never to take good times or wellbeing for granted. This perspective is important to me and the reason why I'll either be out on my bike or running on Sunday mornings, rather than opening my laptop.

Actively acknowledging our own vulnerability to stress and working on strategies to counter this are really important – particularly when working in a challenging environment. In areas of high deprivation, when facing ongoing external scrutiny or at times of significant change, it is inevitable that the level of challenge and stress will be higher. Failing to acknowledge and work deliberately on our wellbeing in these situations is like trying to walk on the moon without a space suit; no one is superhuman.

By no means can I say that I've cracked it, but I love my work and I am usually happy to put in long hours, with strategies in place to avoid it getting unhealthy again. They say that what doesn't kill you makes you stronger and I believe this to be true in most cases.

Thankfully, through support from my family and time with a counsellor, I learned about various wellbeing tools and techniques, such as cognitive behavioural therapy (CBT) and mindfulness, which helped me through. Although difficult, this experience helped me to build resilience to cope better with challenges in the future.

If you are reading this and recognise some of the same unhealthy habits in yourself, do yourself a favour and get some help to get it all in order – make it a priority. If you are reading this and haven't experienced it, you could do worse than to work on some wellbeing tools anyway, as everyone is vulnerable – particularly in the high-stress roles that working in some schools can involve.

Introspection

1. Do you recognise any of the symptoms of burnout in yourself?

2. Could you find a mentor or coach to support you in school?

3. Have you identified the positive aspects of your day in school?

4. Does your use of social media drain or inspire your teaching?

5. Can exercise play a bigger role in your life?

6. Have you tried mindfulness to combat feelings of stress?

CHAPTER 9
TOO QUIET TO TEACH?

I think introverts can do quite well. If you're clever you can learn to get the benefits of being an introvert, which might be, say, being willing to go off for a few days and think about a tough problem, read everything you can, push yourself very hard to think out on the edge of that area
Bill Gates

"I was told in my NQT year that I would never make it as a teacher – I was far too quiet." Such comments are depressingly common. So many teachers have contacted me to express frustration that their quietness is perceived as a barrier to effective teaching. Many of these talented educators nearly gave up on their dream to teach because of the opinions of others.

So, is there any truth in such comments? Are some people just too quiet to enter the teaching profession? In this chapter we will examine why such claims are entirely misguided and overlook the special qualities that quieter teachers bring to the classroom.

Personality feedback
Megan Price (@teachermeg_n), an English NQT, wrote to me about her experience: "On my PGCE, I was told to develop my 'teacher voice' and that I should be 'more sassy'. This bothered me because it didn't strike me as useful pedagogical advice, more a reflection of my mentor's ideal personality in the classroom." This begins to encapsulate what is wrong with character driven feedback.

The implication is that quietness will automatically mean a lack of effectiveness in the classroom, but what message does this send? Does this tell quieter people who are passionate about their subject and about working with children that their contribution is welcome and valuable? We all know that the initial years of teaching can be challenging and sometimes lonely, so we need to nurture teachers at the start of their careers, not criticise them for their personality type.

Laura Tsabet (@lauratsabet), now a lead practitioner at The Bourne Academy in Bournemouth, has found that her quiet temperament has not prevented her from thriving in education. But, despite her talent, she was initially rejected from teacher training:

> "I had two years of experience volunteering in a secondary school when I applied for the PGCE the first time around. I was certain that it would make me stand out from the rest of the candidates and would work in my favour when I could talk about it at interview. But I was turned down. The leader of the course told me she didn't think I had the confidence to be a teacher, that I was perhaps a little too quietly spoken.
>
> Disheartened, I went away and worked as a TA for a year before applying to the same PGCE course the following year. This time I was accepted but told I might need to work on my 'teacher voice' if I wanted to succeed. My family and friends all seemed shocked that I would want to be a teacher in a secondary school. 'But you're so shy and small,' I was often told. 'Aren't you afraid they'll be bigger than you?'
>
> Undeterred, I went ahead with the course anyway, impressing schools and shocking the PGCE leader, who said it was like seeing a different person in the classroom. I'm still an introvert. I'm still shy in groups and particularly when meeting new people. But I'm a fantastic teacher and I feel confident in my teaching abilities. I just hope that other introverts like me haven't had the same experiences and been put off such a worthwhile career."

Laura has demonstrated perseverance and an innate confidence in her own abilities – something that quieter teachers need to cultivate in order to overcome negative and wrongheaded perceptions.

Quiet strengths

Some people assume that children will fail to connect with a quieter teacher. They are completely mistaken. Extroversion is not an essential part of the teacher toolkit and students need to understand that teachers are not created in an extrovert factory. We are people and we represent wider society: some of us are gregarious, some are funny, some are loud and, of course, some are quiet.

Rather than seeing temperament as a barrier to effective classroom practice, we should consider how quieter teachers can thrive in schools. We don't need to advocate a personality change. Rather, we need to identify how quieter teachers can work effectively without altering who they are.

First, we need to recognise the many strengths of quieter teachers. The list is long: reflective skills; interpersonal skills; a dislike of conflict that can facilitate calm classrooms; drive and focus; a passion for their subject; and, perhaps most important of all, a deep empathy for their students and colleagues.

Subject knowledge

If a teacher is quiet outside the classroom, it doesn't necessarily follow that this persona will be presented in the classroom. Many quieter teachers have told me that they become an exaggerated, more extroverted version of themselves in front of their students.

That extroversion can be most readily channelled when sharing a passion for learning and a passion for a subject. Introverted individuals often have a narrower range of interests, but that means we possess extensive knowledge of our subject. Showing our students how passionate we are about a topic or an idea we are exploring with them is one way to help them connect to our lessons. These words, from Oliver Sacks's autobiography *On the Move: A Life*, are interesting in terms of guiding how we behave in the classroom:

"I am shy in ordinary social contexts; I am not able to 'chat' with any ease; I have difficulty recognizing people (this is lifelong, though worse now my eyesight is impaired); I have little knowledge of and little interest in current affairs, whether political, social, or sexual. Now, additionally, I am hard of hearing, a polite term for deepening deafness. Given all this, I tend to retreat into a corner, to look invisible, to hope I am passed over … But if I find someone, at a party or elsewhere, who shares some of my own (usually scientific) interests – volcanoes, jellyfish, gravitational waves, whatever – then I am immediately drawn into animated conversation."

Lessons give us the opportunity to bedazzle, engage and inspire. This is how we encourage students and get them interested in our subjects, by slowly revealing our knowledge and enthusiasm. Lessons allow quieter teachers to escape the monotony of everyday chat and become immersed in the worlds we are deeply interested in.

Strategic planning

Introverts have, as we have already explored, a keen eye for detail and the capacity for deep focus. This ability to work without distraction, and to even enjoy doing so, can be channelled into strategic planning that aims to build progressively on young people's curriculum skills. Such planning can help to reduce teachers' feelings of stress. We can also think carefully about how much noise and collaboration we want: having some quieter lessons or parts of the day will help to make school life more manageable.

The big performance

For many introverted teachers, there is real pleasure in delivering an extroverted performance in the classroom. A degree of freedom comes with presenting a different side of our characters. It is one of the aspects of teaching that I love: in front of a class I am stripped of the inhibitions I often feel in everyday conversations. I am free to present a more vivacious and dynamic aspect of my personality.

We also understand, of course, that our students require a certain level of extroversion in order to get them "on side", both in terms of connecting with us as individuals and engaging with our material. It is why humour, energy and enthusiasm are so potent and powerful in the classroom.

Working with young people requires us to be a supercharged version of ourselves – one that may not be instantly recognisable to those who know us best. The Cambridge professor Brian Little has suggested that we can act out of character in order "to advance a core project in our lives". Little has shared how he is able to move beyond his introversion and connect with his students as a professor. "I adore my students and I adore my field and I can't wait to tell them about what's new and exciting," he said. "So I act in an extroverted way." In other words, he added, "I profess."

However, it is vital here to remember the earlier points about burnout: adopting a more fluid persona can be draining for teachers. We need to be aware that we are "performing" more than other teachers might, and thus allow ourselves the time and space to recuperate.

We have seen the undeniable benefits that a quiet approach to the classroom can bring. But introverted teachers also need a degree of assertiveness. It would be naive to expect students to automatically follow our every instruction, be it quietly delivered or not, and for quieter teachers this can be an issue. We are averse to conflict and confrontation – this is a good thing, but we need to be able to assert our authority. In the next chapter, we will explore quiet behaviour management...

A quiet reflection

Adrian Bethune (@AdrianBethune) is a primary teacher and the author of Wellbeing in the Primary Classroom: A Practical Guide to Teaching Happiness.

When I switched careers to become a primary school teacher back in 2010, having enjoyed a decent stint working in music publishing, I quickly came to the conclusion that teaching maybe wasn't for me. I found the transition really hard, and feelings of stress and anxiety kept me up most nights and stopped me enjoying being in the classroom. I got to the end of most days desperate for my class to go home, so I could savour the quiet of an empty classroom. 'You can't be cut out for the classroom if you can't wait to be rid of your class,' I often thought to myself.

But around this time I read a book called *Quiet* by Susan Cain, which explores how introverts can thrive in a world designed for extroverts. I reflected that my wanting my class to go home was actually a sign that I was overstimulated by my teaching day and that I needed to make some changes to suit me better. Luckily, I'd started a mindfulness course outside of school and so I introduced a short meditation practice with my class straight after register. It made the mornings so much calmer (and quieter!). I made sure that at lunchtime I took a stroll around the block by myself – it really did help me recalibrate after the morning and prepare for the afternoon. I also incorporated silent periods into every lesson, in which the children got on with independent work.

These small tweaks made a big difference. No longer did I feel overwhelmed by the end of the day. I felt like I had more energy and my class were also benefiting from the quieter classroom. There were fewer fallouts and tussles over glue sticks, and a greater focus in lessons. The quiet revolution had begun and, slowly but surely, it started to spread in my school. But you had to be really quiet to notice it.

Introspection
1. Are you aware of the strengths you possess as an introverted teacher?

2. Do you use your ability to focus and plan to your advantage?

3. Do you share your deep interest in your subject with your students?

4. Do you appropriately present a more extroverted persona to engage and motivate young people?

CHAPTER 10
QUIET BEHAVIOUR
MANAGEMENT

The best answer to anger is silence
Marcus Aurelius

I was dreadful at maths at school. I languished in the bottom sets and came very close to not achieving the pass at 16 that I needed to eventually become a teacher. As an adolescent, there is a corrosive bottom-set mindset that can have a profound impact on your confidence and efficacy as a learner. You begin to think that if you represent the worst in the year in one subject, then by default you must be poor at the others.

As with all trials and tribulations, positives eventually emerge. There is no doubt in my mind that my experience has influenced my manner in the classroom: I can empathise with the struggle many students experience in my own subject. It is why I believe that the language we use to talk about motivation and ability is so important.

There were, on reflection, two reasons for my mathematical misery. The first, I can see now, was my single-minded introverted nature. I didn't like numbers; I liked words. Numbers felt alien in every single way (I will never understand how I ended up marrying an economist!). The only way I could begin to solve the puzzles that perplexed me was by working through them at home, poring over the workbooks and trying to make sense of them in my own head. In class, the minute someone started talking to me about numbers or equations, I would drift off – usually into a book-themed daydream.

The second reason was the teacher, a tyrannical woman who was certainly not familiar with the adjective "quiet". She ruled her classroom through fear. She would scream and shout her way through lessons, while I quivered and sought refuge in anything but the maths in front of me. I needed the mental space to process mathematical problems, but that space was filled with anxiety about being caught out and berated for my limited knowledge.

Interestingly, I recently read Craig Barton's book *How I Wish I'd Taught Maths* and was immensely inspired and engaged throughout. This could have been my introverted CPD and learning coming to fruition, or perhaps it was down to Craig's boundless energy and good humour. He could have taught my school maths teacher a thing or two.

Ruling by fear

I shared that anecdote about my school days for a purpose, not just as some warped form of edu-therapy. It shows that the atmosphere created by teachers in their classrooms has a significant impact on learners.

In my career, I have been in schools and classrooms that were ruled by an iron fist. Corridors echoed with the sound of teachers' raised voices and there was a constant feeling of being on edge. This is an atmosphere that stifles lots of young people, but it has a particularly detrimental impact on quieter students. Their stimulation and anxiety levels rocket, diminishing the clarity they need to think carefully.

As an NQT, I believed I had to raise my voice and did some pretty accurate impressions of Groundskeeper Willie, the angry Scottish janitor in *The Simpsons*. My view now, as a student and as a teacher, is that shouting serves only to intimidate and limit the capacity for deep thought. Indeed, it often backfires spectacularly, as louder, more aggressive students reciprocate with the same behaviour.

As the adults in the room, we have a duty to model behaviour that is more sophisticated and befitting of our life experience and maturity. The damage that roaring with anger can do is considerable, shattering relationships, confidence and classroom learning dynamics. The solution, as we shall see, is something much quieter.

A quieter style

There is an old adage, whispered in staffrooms, that quieter teachers make for quieter classes. A stroll around a school building will often provide much evidence to support this adage, with some classrooms appearing to be a utopian world of calm and concentration. The issue, however, is that the secrets of this quiet success are rarely shared with those of us who need them most. The modest natures of these teachers make them unlikely to speak about their own practice.

What are these teachers doing in their classrooms and what can we learn from them? This chapter will seek to open up those classroom doors and get to the heart of quieter behaviour management.

Cool, calm and collected

Our students, for good and for bad, spend many hours a week in our company, so our potential to influence them is huge. Students find it very challenging to sustain heightened emotion in the face of eerie calm, and quieter teachers often have a cool, collected demeanour that can help to defuse even the most difficult situations.

Our voices are a remarkably important and under-discussed aspect of our teaching. Variation, intonation and pitch can heavily influence the dynamic and behaviour of a class. The scores of individuals who were put off teaching by the accusation that their voices were too quiet may, in fact, have been on to a behavioural winner.

A number of teachers have the opposite problem: they talk far too loudly. In the face of distractions and inattention, they ramp up the volume, which in turn causes the students to get even louder. These teachers are usually exhausted at the end of the school day.

Young people, for all their wonderful qualities, are not full of patience. If a teacher's volume is misjudged, students will groan, shrug and artfully ignore. But the softly-softly approach can have the desired effect: turn down the volume and students will lean in, often more attentive and engaged. These reflections, from David Bishop (@wayrf) of Stanborough School in Hertfordshire, offer a helpful analysis of this:

"The more I teach, the less I use my voice. Or rather, I use my voice more effectively, for actually *teaching* pupils rather than reprimanding them. In the past couple of years, I've discovered the power of non-verbal behaviour management: the targeted use of looks, hand gestures and movement around the classroom. It's amazing how effective just standing close to a potential troublemaker can really be. Sometimes, you don't even have to do anything else.

When I first started teaching, my immediate instinct would be to raise my voice, to effectively shout across the classroom. It's something I witnessed my NQT mentee doing, and I think it comes from a lack of confidence, fear and a desire to shut situations down immediately. Sometimes, it is necessary, especially when pupil safety is at risk – but I was doing it far too much. Not only did it show me overreacting and losing control (when I desperately wanted to hang on to it), but it also broke the mood of the classroom. Loud voices aren't conducive to writing in silence, whoever they belong to.

Now, having also got better at anticipating situations, I'm a firm believer in the quiet word, the pointed finger and wide-eyed look of surprise when a pupil isn't doing what they should be. Most of the time, the majority of the class are unaware it's happening, and it also doesn't show pupils up and give them a situation they have to face up to. For while talk is cheap, silence is golden."

As David eloquently highlights, quiet behaviour management can be simple and effective. As well as vocal volume, what are the other aspects of this approach?

- **Move less.** As we shall see in a later chapter, young people's ability to concentrate is being eroded by technology and the pace of modern life. Teachers need to do everything in their power to sharpen that concentration. It is interesting to experiment with movement in the classroom: when we need to make a point about conditions in the room, standing still and being very intentional with our movement helps. Stillness can also be employed when we set a class off on a task: keep your classroom environment quiet and focused by standing serenely at the front of the room and saying, "I am going to watch for two minutes to make sure we all settle well into this task."

- **Speak deliberately.** Talking less means that students know they need to listen when quiet teachers do speak. You can signal your intention with phrases like, "I need pens down and full attention while I make an important point." When employed judiciously, this encourages students to lean in and listen.

- **Model calm.** Given the rapid change taking place in young people's brains, they lack the capacity to regulate their emotions as effectively as adults. We all know students who flare up at the merest provocation. Teachers can be a powerful influence and can have a real impact by modelling calm, restrained behaviour.

Eleanor Mears (@EnglishEffects), a head of English who runs the blog myenglisheffects.com, wrote to me about how she uses her quieter voice to good effect in the classroom:

"As a student in primary and secondary school, I can still remember the teachers who made me feel frightened and those who affected my mental health growing up, because of their aggressive behaviour.

I have the privilege of being appointed in a 'pivotal school', where teachers are expected not to shout and where a restorative approach to behaviour for learning, based on the work of Paul Dix, is taken. I have never been a 'loud' teacher; I consider myself firm, but fair. As a young teacher, I was told by a senior leader to stop being 'so ambitious' and that there was no need to 'rush' as I ought to develop a more confident voice before being considered for promotion.

I am pleased that I ignored this advice! I do not believe that having a loud voice is akin to having a strong presence in the classroom. Students feel safe with clear boundaries and routines and, in my experience, relationships are at the heart of successful teaching."

Building relationships

What can we learn from more introverted teachers about building effective relationships? First, let's consider their capacity to notice and remember details and information about young people. Just like the deliberate and correct use of their name, this signals that you care about them as an individual – they are more than just a grade on a spreadsheet.

This can pay huge dividends. Kate Lowdon (@Miss_Lowdon), a science teacher from the North East of England, told me the following: "I think the power of observation and reflection can be a huge advantage for 'introverts'. I've been overwhelmed with thank-you cards from students this year noting how they have appreciated me remembering the little things and noticeably going the extra mile!"

Building effective relationships also requires a degree of appropriate warmth. We've all heard the phrase "don't smile until Christmas", but this is a misconception. We need to show young people that they matter and we are pleased to see them. A smile can help to achieve this, even if it requires an Oscar-worthy performance on a Friday afternoon!

Our use of language is crucial: do we signal positivity, or do we begin berating young people the minute they enter our classrooms? Do we take the time to deliver a quiet piece of praise? As Paul Dix highlights in his book *When the Adults Change, Everything Changes: Seismic Shifts in School Behaviour,* taking the time to contact home can be worthwhile: "At the top of the hierarchy of recognition is acknowledgement that communicates positive messages to the child's home. The positive note is high level recognition. Perhaps just one child from the class will earn that note, and perhaps some weeks there will be no one."

Being assertive

In any discussion about behaviour management, it is important to not be naive. The reality is that no teacher – quiet or loud – is effective in the classroom without the ability to assert their authority. Can quieter teachers do this? A senior leader contacted me online to share the following about one of his staff members: "I interviewed a small lady with a quiet voice. During her interview I asked her about her classroom presence, looking for a self-assured, confident answer. What I got was the best answer ever: 'I may be small and quiet but I'm a lion in MY classroom.' Best appointment I ever made."

History provides us with many examples of people who have been bold and assertive despite their quieter natures. Mahatma Gandhi, for instance, who led India's independence movement, was a pioneer of passive, non-violent resistance. Another notable example is Rosa Parks, the African-American woman who refused to give up her seat on the bus for a white man. Her act of quiet resistance made her a hero of the civil rights movement. So, how do we unleash our own inner lion?

- **Insist on silence**. There is no more obvious, and no more important, quiet strategy. But waiting for absolute quiet can require nerves of steel and certainly doesn't come naturally at first. Jessica Sellers, a KS2 humanities and drama teacher, had this to say about how she persevered despite her quieter nature: "I was told to use it to my advantage. My mentor knew I liked films so told me to be more like Clint Eastwood…everyone has to stop and listen to pay attention."

- **Body language**. Ideally, your body language is always open and non-confrontational, especially in volatile situations. Lessen the tension by pausing to allow a young person to consider their actions before giving sanctions.

- **Conflict response**. Quiet assertiveness is particularly effective in the face of conflict. Refusing to raise your own voice is the first step in calming a young person down. Eye contact is vital in order to signal that their actions are unacceptable.

- **Clear instructions**. Commands can be delivered quietly, but the language cannot be tentative. Make sure there is no doubt about what you want to happen next. Try instructions that begin "I need you to…", "In five minutes, I will see…", "You should be…" and "You must be…". In the words of Dix, "It is certainty that is at the heart of all exceptional behaviour practitioners. Many confuse this with strictness or being tough. They couple it with huge sanctions and crushing punishment. But anger and aggression is unnecessary; certainty is powerful enough on its own."

• **Routine and predictability.** Young people may be coming to school from homes in which stability and structure are not provided. A quiet teacher and quiet classroom environment can help to provide this dependability. Luckily, introverted teachers usually like structure, too. "Silent starters" and "do-now tasks" require students to enter the classroom and complete a task in silence. This helps to settle them and focus their attention. Or your routine might involve predictable lesson endings: my students often stand behind their chairs to answer an "exit question" about the content of the lesson. This doesn't have to be draconian – it can be fun!

Restorative conversations

Working with young people inevitably involves conflict and tension. Tempers may flare and learning will be interrupted. If we don't seek out the root cause of these behaviours, the risk is that they will reoccur, causing significant disruption to learning. So it is important to discuss a child's behaviour with them after an incident.

This takes time, but it makes clear the impact of the student's choices and how they affected the class. It also allows us to set boundaries for the next lesson, which can enable a fresh start for the young person and for us. This helps to keep the relationship as positive and focused on learning as possible.

It is energy-sapping, it is demanding, but we should never have any doubts about our capacity to manage a group of young people. They can sense hesitation or doubt, so we have to be emotionally ready. Using the performance aspect of teaching to present a quiet yet steely demeanour could help classroom behaviour to be more positive and more consistent.

A quiet reflection

This reflection comes from a teacher who asked to remain anonymous. She works at a further education college where she leads GCSE English resits. She often works with students who have a range of behavioural needs and have spent a significant amount of time out of mainstream education.

I was frequently told I was too quiet to teach during my SCITT year (even by my mum, who is a retired teacher). My mentor said I'd need to find a nice, quiet, private sixth-form to work in, which was the exact opposite of what I wanted. I remember googling "introverted teachers" in desperation.

I generally found my teacher training really helpful and I have a lot of respect for the people who trained me. I just found it very frustrating that an extroverted personality was generally seen as the default mode for being a successful teacher. I did manage to find some really positive introverted role models, though. One teacher at the school in which I trained spent all his lunchtimes alone in his classroom, so I asked if I could observe him teaching. Another teacher, who I really admired for her behaviour management in particular, was at the quieter end of the scale and I was really reassured when she said she'd been terrible at behaviour management when she started.

I've been trying to gather my thoughts about a quiet behaviour management style and I'm not sure I have anything revolutionary to say. But during and after my training I did deliberately set out to work out how I could use the strengths of being an introvert (as set out by Susan Cain in *Quiet*) to make my classroom management better/more comfortable for me day-to-day. In what I'm about to say, it's not that I think extroverted people can't do these things, but that I think introverts can find strength in the idea that these might be things they're particularly well suited to.

It's a bit of a cliché but I think building relationships really is key. I'm lucky to have quite small groups where I am, so when students first arrive, often massively lacking in confidence because they've been told they've "failed" their GCSE, I try to sit with each of them for a few minutes and just listen, while they tell me about their educational experience so far and why they think things didn't work out. I think, in Cain's framework, this would fit with an introvert's tendency to gather information and focus intently on meaningful interactions with individuals.

I try to stay calm *all the time* and I never raise my voice, to the point where students often comment on the fact that I never get annoyed. When I was training, my calmness was criticised. But now, when I've got students telling me about how stressed and anxious they were in school, I think the least helpful thing I could do is shout and get annoyed. Again, I think this fits with Cain's description of introverted leadership and the idea that confidence can be communicated by quietness. I'm not saying this is the only way to do things, but I found it helpful to rethink one of my introvert characteristics as a strength rather than a weakness.

I think the main thing then is just relentlessly reinforcing the routines and enforcing a quiet classroom – sweating the small stuff. I really can't cope with too much stimulation (I keep classroom displays to a minimum and keep surfaces clear). This isn't anything new, but I think, again, introverts have a natural "in" to this sort of thing, if we go with Cain's depiction of introverts as often good at being well-prepared and paying attention to detail. Once those small things are dealt with and the general tone of calmness and quiet is set, then everything builds from there.

I also took on board what Cain said about acting the extrovert when necessary. I'll put on a performance of being silly or bossy or grumpy if I think it will help with a lesson/situation. When I was training, I felt forced into it, but now I see it as part of my "introvert" toolkit that I can apply when I want to, but it's not something I have to do to make things work.

Recently, I was shortlisted for TES FE Teacher of the Year, which seemed a bit of a miracle just five years after feeling like my entire personality might be wrong for teaching! I keep thinking of myself as a trainee and how helpful it might have been to know that you can be quiet and still be OK at this.

Introspection

1. Do you set clear and consistent behavioural conditions for students?

2. Do you model the ideal behaviours and signal when students do this well?

3. Do you use your voice to its full potential, experimenting with pitch and tone?

4. Is your communication with students clear and assertive?

5. Do you seek to repair and rebuild relationships through restorative conversations?

CHAPTER 11
TAKING OWNERSHIP OF
TEACHER IMPROVEMENT

*There is only one corner of the
universe you can be certain of improving,
and that is your own self*
Aldous Huxley

Professional development for teachers often seems designed specifically for extroverts. Let's take a typical Inset day. The proceedings open with a whole-staff breakfast at 8.30am. Next comes a carousel of group workshops, led by speakers with plenty of collaborative activities up their sleeves. There is an interactive "warm-up" for the audience, or perhaps some role play (my personal nightmare).

Each session includes a PowerPoint presentation and a significant amount of didactic talking. There is time for group work or discussion (as with our students, this often drifts into chit-chat). After a sociable whole-staff lunch comes an afternoon of departmental time, which involves collaborative lesson planning and more discussion about the morning sessions.

Time alone? Time to reflect or evaluate individually? Not likely.

At the end of such a day, quieter staff are rarely full of motivation and enthusiasm. Rather, they are exhausted and overwhelmed. Training days often require a level of interpersonal performance that goes beyond what is demanded in the classroom. And it is a further strain that these days often occur directly after a school holiday. We are neither prepared for, nor do we particularly desire, such intense communication on the first day back at work.

Inset days
There are, of course, ways to make these training days more bearable – and productive – for teachers with quieter dispositions. Just like in our lessons,

moments need to be built in for meaningful reflection. And it is essential to allow time for a proper lunch break in which teachers have a chance to process the information that has been delivered.

Variation is also useful. Dr Elizabeth Mountstevens (@DrMountstevens), a science teacher at Sir John Lawes School in Harpenden and a self-confessed introvert, told me that her ideal form of CPD was delving into some reading on education. She said she always enjoyed the second of her school's training days, in which staff work on a learning project:

"The projects were originally called Learning Groups. Every member of staff chose an area of practice to develop, and we were put into small groups of about five people working on a similar area. We met during the launch of the groups and a couple of times later in the year for a few minutes each time.

We were encouraged to read or observe colleagues and then presented our findings in a 'marketplace' activity at the end of the year. On paper, this doesn't sound like CPD designed for introverts, but what I liked about it was the flexibility. I chose to get new ideas through reading and was able to try things out and reflect on my practice. One of the things that most suited me was that I was able to generate ideas and reflect on my own, rather than in the busy environment of an Inset day. From what I have read, I think this preference is typical of introverts.

I also found the collaborative aspect manageable, because it was broken into smaller chunks and you could prepare for it. I am among those introverts who are happy to talk about things that matter to them, and the evidence does suggest that collaboration is important in developing your practice. One of my projects was actually on educating introverts.

Recently, the school has adjusted the format slightly to reduce the group aspects and they have been renamed Learning Projects. We have been encouraged to look at the evidence about what works in the area of practice we are developing and the final marketplace has been changed to a group discussion."

This kind of project has real value, not only for more introverted teachers, but also for developing the pedagogical understanding of all teachers. It allows for deeper and more complex exploration of an aspect of teaching. The dissemination of findings and expertise throughout a staff community is also very useful.

But the real question is: just how effective is "louder" professional development? One-off Inset days or guest-speaker CPD (which costs an awful lot of money) are the dominant forms of ongoing training. And, in some cases, they are the only ways in which teachers are encouraged to engage with their development.

Are these methods of enabling teacher improvement actually helpful and meaningful, or are they superficial quick fixes? After all, teaching is a nuanced, skilled and complex profession, so should we be investing more intellectual energy in trying to work towards expert level? Would engaging with our profession in a more profound and intelligent way help to give it the stature it deserves in society?

This chapter will argue that, in order to deepen our pedagogical understanding, we need to take the quiet approach: reflection, evaluation and time. But recommendations for changes in practice should, of course, be grounded in solid evidence. So, what does the latest educational research tell us about effective professional development?

The research

In 2019, I completed a master's degree in practitioner enquiry. For my dissertation, I spent what felt like a ludicrous amount of time reading the educational research on CPD. I wanted to look at the factors that motivate and retain teachers in their first five years in the classroom. Recent government data shows that the percentage of teachers leaving the profession after five years is 33%. That figure is from England, but the retention of teachers is very much a global issue.

To delve into this topic further, I surveyed more than 150 teachers in the first five years of their careers, to find out why so many people leave the profession and what systemic changes are necessary. One of my key findings concerned professional development. We all want to feel we have the space, time and energy to learn and hone our practice. Yet the feedback I got from teachers in their first five years suggested that schools were getting this wrong. Introvert or extrovert, the teachers I spoke to recognised that quick fixes did not deepen their teaching practice. They expressed real frustration over having to engage in superficial CPD that did not relate to their own development needs.

The educational research certainly supports my findings. The results of the Organisation for Economic Co-operation and Development's 2013 Teaching and Learning International Survey (TALIS) showed that this type of CPD was still the most frequently offered in schools – in England, at least. TALIS asks teachers and school leaders about working conditions and learning environments at their schools in order to provide an international comparison.

A report published by the Centre for Education Research and Policy, entitled *Effective Continuing Professional Development for Teachers*, suggests this alternative: "Schools need organisational structures and managements that encourage and facilitate on-going professional learning, rather than focusing on monitoring and regulation." This, however, appears to be less and less common.

The argument that sustained, reflective, *quieter* teacher training has a greater impact is also supported by other research. In their review of CPD that led to improved student outcomes, Timperley et al (2009) found that CPD needed to last for at least a year: "Extended time frames and frequent contact were probably necessary because, in most core studies, the process of changing teaching practice involved substantive new learning that, at times, challenged existing beliefs, values, and/or the understandings that underpinned that practice." This bolsters the claim that isolated CPD sessions deepen understanding only superficially and have a weak impact on classroom teaching.

The theory that collaboration improves teacher practice is debated in the research. Sims and Fletcher-Wood, in their detailed analysis of the research into CPD (2018), wrote: "Large group PD [professional development] is unlikely to be effective, since teachers with different levels of skill require different types of professional development. There is therefore currently an absence of evidence for, as well as evidence against, the claim that collaboration is a characteristic of effective professional development."

So, how might schools support staff to engage with the idea of teaching as an intellectual profession in which they can continually improve? And, perhaps more importantly, how can teachers themselves take greater ownership of their development?

Differentiation

In any school staff, there is a wide range of expertise and needs. Differentiation can be challenging, but schools could prioritise making each member of staff aware of a CPD programme designed for their specific needs. Staff could also be given a choice in how they work on their development. Teachers need a clear rationale for CPD: building in choice will help to provide them with this and put them in the driver's seat.

Reading for CPD

There has been an explosion in the number of blogs and books written by teachers, for teachers. Each provides a window into a practitioner's thought processes and how they work in the classroom. As a form of CPD, they can be invaluable. They allow us to work through insights into classroom practice at our own pace, experimenting with ideas and concepts as we go. We can approach them in whichever way works best for us: through annotation and note-taking, or just through reading for pleasure.

Such reading also provides respite from the interpersonal demands of the day, restoring that desire to learn and improve. Helpfully, the authors have also analysed and provided clarity on a range of educational research. Research is, of course, important in helping us to make informed decisions in the classroom, but it can be almost impossible to find time to make sense of complex research articles in a full teaching timetable.

As well as reading about teaching, writing about it can be a powerful way to crystallise thinking about what works and what doesn't work. Doing this for an audience, perhaps via a blog, can boost motivation and provide a sense of purpose: if just one teacher gains something from our content, then we are doing something worthwhile.

Podcasts

As a fully fledged introvert, I did a terrible job when I was invited to speak on an Australian podcast. I also, unfortunately, had never listened to a podcast, so I had no idea what to expect. But I found the medium interesting and recognised the scope it offered for the kind of in-depth discussion that introverts connect with. Since then, I have been able to start a podcast for teachers through TES.

The role of interviewer, rather than interviewee, sits better with my disposition and I have had monthly conversations with a range of teachers. For me, these conversations are a chance to discover how an aspect of my teaching can be improved – chances that can be hard to come by in the frantic rush of a working day.

Listening to the reflections of a practitioner with expertise and insight can be a really useful way to engage in "quiet" CPD. My podcasting has encouraged me to try to find opportunities for knowledge-sharing in the school environment – in every school are colleagues with covetable wisdom and expertise.

Coaching

In recent years, an increased understanding of the complexity of teacher improvement has led to a greater focus on the value of coaching and mentoring. The teachers I interviewed in the first five years of their careers spoke of the extensive support they received during their PGCE and NQT year, and of what one described as a "void of individual feedback" afterwards. Although being reflective and taking ownership of our own development will improve our teaching, we all, regardless of experience, need feedback.

Coaching meets the needs of quiet teachers much better than didactic, instructional forms of CPD. It provides them with individual and personalised feedback, and the chance to talk about what matters most to them: how to improve what happens in their classroom.

It is important to highlight the distinction between mentoring and coaching. Mentoring is a more formal process that implies an expert/novice relationship. It is often delivered by a senior manager, has a greater focus on career development and involves passing on advice. In contrast, coaching is action-focused and involves non-directive advice. It is usually more concerned with teaching practice, rather than career development, and the coach can be anyone within the school environment. In short: coaching is about supporting people to find their own solutions.

Not only can coaching help with classroom pedagogy, and provide a means by which staff can investigate good practice, but it can also support wellbeing. Teaching can be a lonely profession and a coach can be a wonderful ally.

Practitioner enquiry

Rather than professional development being mandated according to targets on a school improvement plan, practitioner enquiry allows teachers to lead their own development. We might decide to focus on a particular aspect of our classroom practice, then spend the year reflecting on and evaluating our progress. If we wish, we can share what we have learned with our colleagues. George Gilchrist, the author of *Practitioner Enquiry*, sent me the following as an introduction to how the process works:

> "**Practitioner enquiry**, along with its similar iteration **collaborative enquiry**, provides teachers and school leaders with a systematic and meaningful way of developing learning and teaching, as well as facilitating embedded and sustainable teacher and school development. Building on the work of Lawrence Stenhouse, and others, it positions teachers as enquirers into their practice and the impact they have on learning. Instead of just encouraging teachers to be '**reflective**', it develops in them skills and dispositions that enable them to act on such 'reflections'. Some of the key aspects of practitioner enquiry aim to promote **teacher agency** and the development of **adaptive expertise**, which they bring to their teaching as well as their professional learning. When embraced properly it empowers teachers to take ownership of their professional learning, so it becomes something **they do**, rather than something **done to** them.

Collaborative by nature, it encourages the establishment of learning cultures across settings, as well as for individual teachers to better understand their impact on the learning of the young people they teach. Within this approach everyone is recognised as a learner, and that learning is grounded very much in the individual contexts in which people are working. When embracing enquiry, teachers are expected to identify the '**learning**' issues that are troubling them, then take steps to enquire into these, by gathering data, looking at research and evidence, talking to colleagues and learners, formulating a research question, then identifying some steps towards improvement, based on this learning. They then implement changes, gathering evidence on the impact as they go. The focus of any enquiry, as well as the collection of data, is small and proportionate. Key to the whole process is that it fits easily into the day-to-day work of teachers and schools, with any changes that produce positive outcomes becoming embedded into practice. Experience and evidence have demonstrated that when undertaken carefully, with sufficient time and support provided, small steps can produce larger impacts, both pedagogical and curricular.

When done well, evidence and research demonstrate the **following benefits** from an enquiry approach: raised achievement and attainment for all learners; the connecting of all key aspects of school development; deeper learning and understanding for all learners, including teachers; small changes having big impacts; the development of evidence- and research-informed practice; the development of collaborative cultures, teacher leadership and dispersed leadership; system leadership facilitated; increased teacher agency and empowerment; more impactful professional learning and a 'reprofessionalising' of the teacher role. There are others, too, and all of these are key to any professional learning approach that has impact for learners and participants, as identified over many years and studies by researchers in this field.

One of the overarching aims of such enquiry approaches is to support the development of **self-improving teachers**, which helps with the development of **self-improving schools** and systems. Through the development of enquiry dispositions, and ways of being, we are repositioning professional learning and school development, and are doing this in a repeatable, systematic and rigorous way, for the benefit of all. By the adoption of such an approach, we also protect teachers and schools from the incessant cascading down of initiatives, and change from above, or outside."

We are all different. Discovering a method of professional development that keeps you positive and motivated is essential for wellbeing. Schools need to offer choice and be reflective about the differing needs of all their staff – as, of course, we should be about the needs of our students.

In the next chapter, we will step out of the classroom and explore how quieter teachers can thrive in the other interpersonal situations that arise in schools. As the science teacher Kate Lowdon says: "I feel very at home in my classroom and wouldn't say I am quiet or lack confidence. But throw me into a meeting and ask me to share my thoughts and ideas… Very daunting indeed!"

A quiet reflection

Dr Kulvarn Atwal (@Thinkingschool2) is the author of The Thinking School: Developing a Dynamic Learning Community. *He is currently executive headteacher of two schools. His doctoral thesis, completed in 2016, examined the factors that influence teacher learning in schools.*

My personal experiences of teacher professional learning over the last 20 years have been dominated by the need to train teachers to be able to implement government initiatives, instead of individualised professional learning opportunities. My research has demonstrated that more learning is potentially undertaken informally by teachers in schools, rather than through the formal opportunities designed for teacher learning. For example, there is greater potential to learn from colleagues in your year group team over the course of a week than from the one-hour professional learning meeting after school.

Therefore, we need to consider the learning environments in schools and evaluate the extent to which they maximise both formal and informal learning opportunities for teachers. An introduction to workplace learning theories elevated my thinking about teacher learning and opened up my eyes to the possibility of creating a far more dynamic learning environment for all teachers within a school. This is central in the thinking school, and fundamental to improving children's learning experiences.

In contrast to the concepts of informal learning, my personal observations of teacher engagement in CPD (I use the term CPL, continued professional learning) were that it seemed neither to deepen learning over time nor to promote collaborative learning among staff. Too much CPL is short-term and not contextualised in practice. I am talking about courses or conferences off-site, usually organised by the local authority. Teachers perhaps valued the opportunity to have a day out of school but the impact back at school was slight, particularly in terms of wider teacher learning or children's learning outcomes. While I was working at a school in 2008 that was deemed to be struggling, representatives of the local authority were particularly dismissive of our intentions to promote teacher learning through action research – that demonstrated to me that there was a lack of wider awareness of the factors that actually influence teacher learning and development.

The situation was the same when I joined my current school as headteacher, a few weeks after it had been categorised by Ofsted as "requiring improvement". I explained my determination and intention that all teachers would develop their understanding of the craft of learning and teaching, and that we would do this through engagement in year-group collaborative-action research projects with learning-focused lesson observations. I was immediately informed that the teachers were not ready for this, and that I needed to observe each teacher and give them a judgement of their teaching (a choice of "unsatisfactory", "requiring improvement", "good" or "outstanding") and then give them targets for improvement. I refused and stuck with my original plan, even though I was told that Ofsted would return within 18 months and it was my job that was on the line. In leadership, you absolutely have to do what you believe is right.

I felt that these attitudes to school improvement were a reflection of the impact of government policy in promoting teacher learning through short-term, externally developed courses. The notion presented by local authority advisors and external consultants was that action research would be "more appropriate" for a school that was in a stronger position and more successful. I was told that it would be better to send teachers on one-day courses entitled "From Good to Outstanding". I am not discounting the fact that teachers can pick up worthwhile strategies from attending a generic course such as this. However, my own experiences are that teacher-learning activities such as these seldom allow sufficient time for teachers to reflect on the impact of any changes introduced on children's learning. Teachers also need to have the tools and the time to develop the skills to undertake this type of reflection effectively. Too many schools and teachers remain dependent on outside intervention to support their professional learning, instead of exploiting the informal and formal learning opportunities available in every school. Many leaders in schools do not have the skills to develop the structures and cultures to promote an expansive learning environment or to develop teachers' professional learning skills, including reflection upon practice. However, I do think all schools are capable of developing into thinking schools.

If, as I advocate we should, we move towards professional learning communities within and across schools, we need to reconceptualise our views on what constitutes effective teacher professional learning. A recent review of international reviews of effective teacher professional learning (Cordingley et al, 2015) has highlighted the significance of sustained learning activities over time that additionally facilitate experimentation in the classroom. This requires us to change our understandings of the role of the teacher. I envisage each teacher in the thinking school to be a potential Master of Education who is actively engaging in research, continually experimenting to improve their craft year on year. If this is taking place within a wider environment of a professional learning community, the impact will be very powerful.

Building a dynamic learning community

My research sought to identify the complex factors that influence teachers' learning experiences in primary schools. I evaluated teachers' perceptions of these factors and drew on them to build a model for the provision of positive formal and informal learning for teachers in primary schools. Key features of this model include specific teacher-learning activities that can be implemented in schools to support formal learning opportunities and encourage informal learning activities within the wider development of a positive and expansive learning environment. Examples of these activities include:

- Opportunities and time made available for teachers to conduct research.

- Opportunities for teachers to select their own focus for professional learning that is related to pupil learning and contextualised in their own practice.

- Opportunities to coach and be coached.

- Opportunities for collaborative working in pairs and teams across different groups within the school.

- Opportunities to engage in peer learning and lesson studies to co-construct knowledge.

- Non-judgemental learning-focused lesson observations.

To enable this model to work successfully, it is imperative that teacher learning is led by learning-focused leaders who are able to work in partnership with teachers and contribute to the learning activities. Through teacher engagement in a dynamic community of learners, they in turn develop the skills of learning-focused leaders. The community itself then continues to innovate, grow and develop. I describe the learning community in the model as dynamic because my work has shown that the development of these key learning activities has a dynamic effect on teacher learning in schools. The structures within the model create a culture that in turn promotes the development of positive attitudes to learning.

All members of staff will become and develop the skills of learning-focused leaders. The word "dynamic" has been used to define both the system within the learning community "characterised by constant change and progress" and the learning-focused leaders who are "positive in attitude and full of energy and new ideas". I have designed a model that I hope will inform the future implementation of teacher-learning activities in primary schools, and promote expansive, personalised formal and informal learning activities. I am passionate in my belief that if you implement this model, you will see a significant positive impact on the learning of all the children in your school.

Introspection

1. Do you engage with CPD only during Inset days and presentations?

2. What mechanisms could you use to become more reflective about your practice?

3. Could you make use of a coach in your teaching environment?

4. Could you set up your own practitioner enquiry? What would it focus on?

5. How could you build in more collaborative approaches to engaging with teacher improvement?

CHAPTER 12
THRIVING OUTSIDE
THE CLASSROOM

I just hate meetings
JK Rowling

At the end of my first fully qualified year of teaching, when I had just turned 26, I was asked to take on an assistant headteacher role in my school in central London. I had no previous management experience (I'm not sure that a few months of managing a running store really count) and no previous responsibility in the school.

The only things that "qualified" me for the role were a strong work ethic and a slightly obsessive focus on teaching and learning. I was functioning as lots of introverted new teachers do: I was hiding in my classroom, investing lots of time and energy in trying to teach effectively, and doing my best to build positive relationships with students. None of it was for show – I was just trying to be a good teacher.

Fortunately – or unfortunately – this was a school with lots of scrutiny: graded lesson observations, book reviews and learning walks. My "outstanding" lessons, constructed with a typical introvert's painstaking attention to detail, attracted the attention of the leadership team. The school had one Ofsted focus point: to develop the overall quality of its teaching and learning. I was to spearhead that mission.

I was grateful for the opportunity, but I should have known that my temperament would make such a leap very challenging. I was about to be catapulted from the comfort of my classroom into a position of whole-school responsibility for which I was entirely unprepared. I gave it a good go, but it was a significant factor in the burnout I experienced two years into the role.

I was lucky that the school noticed leadership qualities in me that might not have been immediately apparent. But many quieter teachers are overlooked and deprived of the chance to take on more responsibility. Instead, as is often the way, those who are louder tend to be given more opportunities.

Being heard

The world outside the classroom can be more intimidating for quieter teachers than many realise. Paula Corbin (@corbin_paula), an English teacher at Bradford College, wrote to me about her experiences in meetings:

> "I receive praise for my 'calm' approach in the classroom, but I am told that I'm 'very quiet' outside of it. To me, this translates as 'you possess a positive trait in the classroom', but outside of it 'you're not expressive enough'.
>
> As an introverted teacher, I embrace and enjoy the interpersonal demands of teaching – in the classroom, with learners who I can genuinely appreciate. I utilise that time to build a rapport with each and every one because it's instinctive to, not because I have to. I feel that being introverted means wanting each learner to feel comfortable and valued, whether they're on the introverted or extroverted side.
>
> On the flip side, outside of the classroom, it's a different narrative. Meetings appear to be a game for the extroverts of the department. Whereas, knowing myself fairly well, I'm aware that I have to feel as though my points add value to the meeting. However, by the time I've reflected on others' points and come to a conclusion that I'm ready to contribute, the meeting is generally over! As a result, it feels as though management perceive me as the 'quiet' one (despite not being). The sad consequence of that is that we've both lost hope for any revival of input from me. I've been given a label and I generally stick with it (regrettably).
>
> Extroverted colleagues also view me as 'the quiet one', advising me to 'speak up' even when there is nothing of importance I want to say. It baffles me that they truly do not understand this. On a positive note, I am able to take myself away to an empty classroom and think, breathe and recharge. The environment I work in allows me to do this intermittently, in between teaching, and without it I would have quit teaching a long time ago. I no longer allow any internal dialogue that I have to speak for the sake of it, because the students are the ones who matter and they benefit with me wanting to do my best for them."

Paula's experience will ring a bell with many teachers. She is another recipient of that infuriating conjunction: but. The implication is that being quieter is a deficiency – there is a lack of recognition of the ways in which introverted teachers contribute successfully. And Paula's reflections raise important questions. How can introverted teachers work within their temperaments to make their voices heard? And what can leaders and managers do to enable them to share their views?

Better meetings

In all the conversations I had with quieter teachers in preparation for this book, their experiences of meetings stood out more than anything else. They expressed feelings of anxiety, exclusion and being out of place. Meetings can have a hugely damaging impact on introverted teachers, crushing self-esteem and making them question their ability to contribute outside of the classroom.

During my masquerade as a senior leader, I had to attend the leadership team's dreaded Monday evening meetings. They were spoken about in hushed tones among the teaching staff; their duration and intensity were legendary. My first Monday evening meeting did nothing to dispel the rumours: it lasted for *five hours*. Unfortunately, that was not a one-off. I spent every one of those meetings in a state of heightened anxiety, praying that nobody would ask me a spontaneous question. Other than when I was explicitly asked to respond or prepare an agenda item, I did not once contribute voluntarily. My anxiety was exacerbated by the size of the meetings: the room was usually packed with 14 staff.

These days, I am noticeably perkier than most of my colleagues on a Monday morning, free from the dread of that epic meeting. But, still, my default mode in a meeting of four or more people is complete silence. I often end up in an internal tussle: I feel under pressure to contribute, but I'm unable to think clearly enough to offer anything that I believe to be of merit.

Why is it that introverts tend to suffer in meetings? The most obvious reason is that larger meetings might as well have been designed for extroverts. There is no one-on-one interaction and little time for individual reflection. And there are several other reasons:

- **The volume.** Meetings can be highly competitive environments in which quieter people find it difficult to interject. It can seem as though everyone else is an extrovert vying hard to be heard; meanwhile, the introverts are agonising over what to say. The irony is that often the most dominant voices contribute the least useful points.

- **The speed.** We have seen that introverted individuals need time to process information and mentally rehearse what they are going to say.

But by the time they have done this, the meeting has usually moved on. Or they have that "Aha!" moment hours after the meeting has concluded – this can be very frustrating.

- **The content.** As we have seen, introverts may have narrower fields of interest and engagement. For example, whenever data is discussed in a meeting, I usually drift into a daydream of an idyllic Highland retreat. As Paula reflected, quieter teachers won't just speak for the sake of it – they need to have something relevant to say before they take the leap. And they are unlikely to feel they can make a meaningful contribution in a discussion that is outside their sphere of expertise.

- **The lack of preparation.** Nothing stresses out introverted individuals more than being put on the spot. If they are asked for a spontaneous and unrehearsed answer, the likelihood is that what they say will not be the best they have to offer.

So, what can quieter individuals do to make meetings a more positive experience? And how can managers alter the process to get the best out of every member of staff? Here are some of the methods that I and other teachers use to navigate the challenge of meetings:

- **Make notes.** An agenda is a powerful thing: if they are distributed in advance of meetings, introverted teachers have time to jot down and rehearse their contributions. This thinking time can help them to see where they can be of value, and the more prepared they feel for a meeting, the more effectively they will be able to communicate.

- **Come back to me.** If you ask a spontaneous question of an introverted teacher in a meeting, stave off their panic by following it up with, "Can you come back to me in a few minutes?" This is never received badly and it gives them an opportunity to reflect and formulate their thoughts. This way, you get the best out of them.

- **Ditch the stimulants.** Pre-meeting anxiety can be heightened by a pre-meeting coffee. In his book *Me, Myself and Us*, Professor Brian Little argues that introverts become less efficient after drinking coffee: "After ingesting about two cups of coffee, extraverts carry out tasks more efficiently, whereas introverts perform less well. This deficit is magnified if the task they are engaging in is quantitative and if it is done under time pressure." A loud, crowded space – such as a school or a meeting – can be similarly debilitating!

- **Get in early**. The longer self-doubt is allowed to linger, the worse it gets. If the end of a meeting is approaching and you haven't yet contributed anything useful, the internal monologue can be so loud that it is almost impossible to form a coherent answer. One of the best things you can do is speak as early as possible in a meeting. It settles the nerves and bolsters confidence.

- **Contribute in writing**. Meetings don't stop when we are no longer in each other's presence – human psychology doesn't work that way. Quieter individuals may consider a meeting long after it concludes and, if they have a sharp moment of clarity, they should know that it is not too late to contribute. We have seen that introverts often find writing a good way to communicate, so a follow-up email or a quick note can be a way for their voice to be heard. Even better are one-on-one conversations after meetings.

Public speaking

Confidence in the classroom does not automatically translate into confidence in other forms of public speaking. In fact, just the thought of it can strike terror into the hearts of some teachers. Yet, despite the anxiety, no teacher should shrink from sharing their practice or contributing to training.

Malcolm Gladwell, the author of *Blink: The Power of Thinking Without Thinking* and a range of other non-fiction books, has said the following about public speaking: "Speaking is not an act of extroversion. People think it is. It has nothing to do with extroversion. It's a performance, and many performers are hugely introverted." He goes on to say that when he speaks, he's inhabiting "a storytelling role that I don't inhabit when I'm not on the stage. I'm not the chatty one at the dinner table or at parties."

Successful public speaking comes down, in part, to preparation. I tend to scribble down what I want to say, then spend some time distilling those notes into a clear structure for the presentation or talk. Finally, they become a series of bullet points that provide comfort and clarity during the "performance".

During the presentation itself, I try to be as relaxed as possible. This can be really hard, but humour can help to relax you and the audience – an anecdote can be a great way to begin a talk. Keep your body language open and remember to smile!

Self-esteem

We have already seen the harm that self-doubt can cause. Doubt and introversion can go hand in hand, with quieter teachers suffering from lower self-esteem and confidence. This is often what holds them back from applying for promotions or even being more vocal in the school environment. The best and most authentic teachers I have come across, however, don't radiate confidence and self-assurance; they radiate instead a questioning spirit. This doubt drives them forward and helps them to provide their very best for young people.

In her book *How to Be Alone*, Sara Maitland makes an important point about the frustration introverts can feel about their personalities: "At the same time as pursuing this 'extrovert ideal', society gives out an opposite – though more subterranean – message. Most people would still rather be described as sensitive, spiritual, reflective, having rich inner lives and being good listeners, than the more extroverted opposites."

The reality is that quieter individuals are more likely to underestimate themselves and be underestimated by others. Eleanor Roosevelt, an introvert who became a UN delegate, human rights activist, teacher and lecturer (she averaged 150 speaking engagements a year) said: "You wouldn't worry so much about what others think of you if you realized how seldom they do."

Self-awareness is vital to growth in any profession. Impostor syndrome is felt by all of us, to a degree, but often it is merely a voice in our heads that prevents us from going for what we want. Instead of being held back by our "deficiencies" (which may be nothing of the sort), we need to work out what will bring us most satisfaction, and that may mean taking on leadership responsibility. In the next chapter, we will see how quieter teachers have the potential to be thoughtful and life-changing leaders.

A quiet reflection

Sophie Minchell (@SophieaMinchell) is an English teacher at Cramlington Learning Village in Northumberland.

Being shy in teaching is an interesting balance. Those who know me would most likely disagree. How can you class as shy someone who demonstrates the traits of being social and confident? However, to the introverted mind, shyness itself is more complex than that. The universal assumptions of timidity and nervousness only graze the surface of what it fundamentally means. It's the private insecurities that are rarely shared. My current veneer of confidence is the result of hard work, practice and determination, rather than an intrinsic personality trait. Unlike when I was younger, I can't run away or avoid situations any more because I find them a threat. Teaching has done wonders for my character: it's made me reflect on my own strengths and weaknesses each day and forced me to deal with my own insecurities.

When I first told people that I was going into teaching, they were sceptical. My sister told me that she thought the kids were going to make mincemeat of me. Another friend refused to believe that I was going into secondary – she said I was too nervous and sensitive. To an extent, during the first year, they were right. I knew I had to be strong, but then it's easy to mistake that for confrontational, which in my normal life I am not. If I get into an argument with anyone, I fret about it for days. I found myself, time and time again, getting into difficult conversations with students and having to deal with it. After all: I am the adult in the situation.

After teaching a student for three years, he told me that he liked that I spoke to them "as equal", rather than "patronising" them. Now, this was an exceptionally intelligent class, with students that have gone on to do wonderful things. It's certainly not an approach that lends itself to lower-ability groups that rely on or find home in familiarity, order and routine. However, I have found that this has worked on many occasions. Showing a vulnerable, introverted side can reap rewards. Being honest and showing a fragile element of character can provide a refreshing realism to what is, in essence, a very artificial environment: 30 students of all backgrounds and characters, all in one room, with an adult who is trying to deliver something that doesn't always feel relevant to them. Showing genuinely human reactions of pride, humour, anxiety or even frustration can be an effective way of validating. Explaining to students that "this sometimes works better for me when I go and sit on my own and have a rest from it and then go back to writing after five minutes" does provide a reasonable way out. The forceful "get it done now" attitude hasn't worked for me and has only ever provoked stress and anxiety. My own reflections as an introvert have informed my day-to-day practice, mainly on the power of empathy.

In my practice, I've tried to avoid the scaremongering that I felt as a student myself. Don't get me wrong: I have definitely, when under pressure, fallen into it. And I have said things and behaved in ways that I know are not good for the most anxious students in the room. But I am *conscious of it*. I am aware that having five lessons a day and not being spoken to is irritating, especially when you see someone for five hours a week.

I've become determined to make an effort to know my students and want them to know that they are seen and recognised in my classroom, whether they're the most confident or the most thoughtful. I don't think this necessarily translates to a "no hands up and pounce" philosophy. I think it's certainly more complex than that. I aim to provide the right *type* of attention to everyone.

My experiences have taught me that there is no "one size fits all" when it comes to getting the best out of students who appear "fine". In a world where we're increasingly replacing verbal communication with computerised responses, I know myself that I have always preferred a human one. I don't need to be forced to speak, as generally I have a lot of ideas in my head that I want to share, but having the right systems in place to share them is necessary. Praise is key. Conversations are, for me, where effective communication lies. Knowing the people in front of me and having a smile ready have helped me out in many a tricky situation.

During the six years of my career, I have been lucky enough to have been surrounded by practitioners who have supported me through what is, in reality, a very difficult career. Teachers naturally want to tell you that you're doing well and are happy to listen. As someone who sometimes doubts myself, being around people who constantly reassure and reflect on themselves has taught me how to self-regulate my worry. Watching people who I regard as teaching gods tell me how difficult a class is, or how they didn't have time to complete everything that day, has taught me the value of sharing my feelings with those around me. It's fine to say that something didn't go well or to share when something really did. It's OK to complain and it's even better to compliment. Reflecting on this staffroom atmosphere and what it has done for me has informed how I deal with things in the classroom. It's OK to say that you struggled with something for the first time or that you really got something. More often than not, the people in front of you feel the same and will feel comforted that they're not the only ones.

I know there's a lot more that I need to do to make everyone comfortable in my classroom. How do you make students, who are intrinsically doubtful, realise that they're good at what they do? I know that I've got it wrong a lot, but I am trying my best to think back to how I felt when I really couldn't do it, but I came to school smiling. The parts of my education that I remember the most are the conversations with my teachers and the reassurances that I wasn't the only one struggling.

Introspection

1. Are you in a position to make meetings easier for your team?

2. What techniques might make meetings more successful for you?

3. What strategies could you employ to improve your public speaking?

4. How can you work alongside natural feelings of self-doubt?

CHAPTER 13
QUIET LEADERSHIP

In a gentle way, you can shake the world
Mahatma Gandhi

Fifty years ago, as he became the first person to walk on the moon, Neil Armstrong uttered the words that would go down in history: "That's one small step for a man, one giant leap for mankind."

Armstrong had a quiet disposition. According to his biographer, James R Hansen, "There was nothing in Neil's personality that really tried to find the limelight. After Apollo 11 he didn't like the celebrity that went with it."

It is a little-known fact that Armstrong was not supposed to be the one to take those historic steps. Tradition dictated that, as commander of the mission, he should have been the last to leave the spacecraft. But the US government felt that Armstrong, with his quiet humility, would be a better representative of America than the extroverted and outspoken Buzz Aldrin. And so it proved: Armstrong fulfilled the role of humble, eloquent hero perfectly.

This is an example of quiet leadership qualities being prized above extroverted tendencies. But, unfortunately, quiet temperaments are often seen as ill-suited to leadership. The prevailing view is that leaders must embody the alpha personality – they must be the bold individuals who thrive centre stage. Job adverts for leadership positions seem to further lionise the extrovert: "dynamic", "motivational" and "enthusiastic" are among the most common descriptors.

This chapter will seek to demonstrate the opposite. It will highlight the downsides of "charismatic" leadership, and show how introverts can make extremely successful leaders.

Leadership traps

If we were a fly on the wall in any staffroom in the land, what criticisms would we hear of school leaders? It doesn't take a genius to guess what might be the most common complaints:

- Lack of attention to detail.

- Arrogance.

- Poor interpersonal skills.

- Lack of effort.

- Stressed and hurried.

And if we were to eavesdrop on staff praising effective leaders, what qualities might they refer to?

- Attention to detail.

- Humility.

- Empathy and listening skills.

- Diligence.

- Calm and measured.

My rather laboured point is that good leadership is not exclusive to extroverts – the innate qualities of introverts can make them wonderful leaders. Claire Stoneman (@stoneman_claire), a deputy headteacher from Birmingham, has written on her blog about the pressure to perform as an extrovert. In one post, she explores her childhood shyness ("I was also shy because I was teased for being clever, so I learnt to shut up in class and not to put my hand up to answer questions") and discusses how she now brings her capacity to listen to her role as a senior leader:

> "This means that sometimes I do much more listening than talking. Conversely, I also talk a lot sometimes. This isn't my default position, but this was often seen as what A Good Leader Should Do in the ten years I've been a senior leader. Have all the answers. Lead from the front. Do all the talking. Be charismatic. I struggled with this when I first became a senior leader, especially as when I first started I couldn't even get the lunch queue sorted.
>
> I thought that as a new assistant headteacher I should be able to do everything with verve and vigour and resolve. That I should stride the corridors and make decisions in a split second, because that's what good, extrovert, charismatic leaders do, right?
>
> I hadn't even considered that there were different ways of doing things, or that different situations called for different knowledge and perhaps a

different approach. Or indeed, that I needed to know stuff very well and practise stuff, and that this was really, really important. This was the X Factor era even in school leadership: if you wanted a school leadership role hard enough then – why! – of course you must have it. It was the epoch of the cult of the individual.

There were some tub-thumping, very vocal school leaders, tiresomely bounding into assembly halls up and down the land. This was when those school values began rolling through laminators and magically appearing on walls overnight: dreaming and believing is all very well, but it's not going to get you far without knowing something, or even simply being aware that you don't know what you don't know."

So, let's move away from the extrovert ideal and unpick why quieter qualities are so powerful in school leadership.

Quiet success

Before training to be a teacher, I spent a year working as a cover supervisor in Whitley Bay High School, a superb school in the North East of England. I was the school's on-site supply teacher, covering lessons when teachers were absent. You can imagine how successful my maths cover lessons were. Luckily, student-led learning was very much in vogue – a trend I ruthlessly exploited!

The role had its challenges, but it taught me a huge amount about schools. It was also an introvert's dream: I could watch, listen and learn from those around me, without the stress and responsibility that are the hallmarks of a training year. And, of course, my watching and listening also applied to the school's leadership team. One of the challenges of leadership is the scrutiny the position attracts, from staff and from students.

The headteacher, Adam Chedburn, was the epitome of a "quiet leader", and was universally respected and admired by the staff – more so than any headteacher I have worked with since. He led Whitley Bay High School for 21 years and became a national leader for education. On retirement, he was appointed OBE for his services to education. So, what was his secret? I contacted Adam when I was writing this book and spoke to him at length about his career. I was fascinated by the way he thought about leadership – he is as far as you can get from the stereotype of the ego-driven leader.

After highlighting that by nature he was "quite shy and really not very good at small talk", Adam spoke about the crucial elements of leadership. He said it was necessary to "surround yourself with people who are better than you, and cherish their ability to do things well". This required courage and an inner confidence, he acknowledged, yet the "inspirational people who fire you up" had sustained him in his headship years. He was keen to point out, however, that "quietness doesn't mean weakness – there needs to be direction and people need to be clear on what expectations are". Leadership, he said, required clarity.

As a leader, Adam's focus was on training and appointing others – on growing outstanding teachers. I was struck by the contrast with much modern school leadership: the "superheads" who are parachuted in and make rapid changes, then vanish before they can see the effect. After I had applied for the job at Adam's school, I was hugely surprised when he telephoned me and invited me to interview, then spent a significant amount of time talking to me – all for a position as a cover supervisor. When I questioned him on this, Adam said he had been deeply involved in appointing staff at all levels. He said that if you are "serious about opportunity for everyone in your school, you need to have outstanding people at all points".

He spoke a great deal about the many skills required by teachers, adding "if you want to be humbled, watch teachers teach". Adam said one of his great pleasures had been watching teachers leave his school and go on to achieve great things in education. The quality of a school, he argued, depended on the investment in relationships.

He also spoke at length about the importance of listening, recognising that headship was a "privileged position" that some heads exploit by wanting to have "the first word and the last word". In leadership team meetings, he "would be the person that said the least", but "what I said was always important".

In our conversation, what resonated most for me was Adam's desire to talk about everyone but himself. He was thoughtful, gracious and celebratory of others. People – other people – were at the heart of his leadership, rather than a need to control, direct and be the best at everything. Adam invested in relationships and built the values of a team. Such an approach can, and should, allow for longevity and pleasure in that most challenging of positions.

After talking to Adam, I reflected further on the benefits of quiet school leadership:

- **Humility**. Quieter individuals often have an aversion to talking about themselves and their achievements. If anything, this can be to their detriment, as it can result in them gaining less recognition than they deserve. In a leadership position, however, humility can be a hugely enabling force. Humble leaders put others first and value their input more – this helps them to build teams and get the best out of people. These leaders are less focused on self-improvement; instead, they strive to have greater impact in their work.

- **Empathy and listening**. In schools, it often feels as if everyone is too overworked and too busy to listen to others. Quiet leaders make time to listen because they know how important it is to understand the experiences of others. In turn, these leaders are listened to when they speak. Positive relationships between staff are, of course, essential in ensuring motivation and efficacy.

- **Hard work**. Rightly or wrongly, leaders are judged on their output. We have already noted the conscientious natures of quiet individuals, whose single-mindedness can lead to exceptional focus and determination. The words of the MP Iain Duncan Smith resonate here: "Never underestimate the determination of a quiet man."

- **Solitude**. Arguably, solitude is a significant component of effective leadership. Stepping back and reflecting carefully can lead to deep understanding, a clear vision and decisions that have real impact. As Jennifer B Kahnweiler, author of *The Introverted Leader: Building on Your Quiet Strength*, has noted, solitude is a powerful tool. "It's kind of like a battery they recharge," she said. "And then they can go out into the world and connect really beautifully with people."

- **Calm**. There is enough emotion and stress in schools without leaders contributing with capricious outbursts. In terms of temperament and tone, it is interesting to consider the differences between Barack Obama and Donald Trump, the former and current presidents of the US. Despite being an exceptional orator, Obama is very much an introvert. His tenure in the White House mirrored his personality: calm, collected and easeful. David Maraniss, the author of *Barack Obama: A Story*, has written that the former president has "a writer's sensibility, where he is both participating and observing himself participating, and views much of the political process as ridiculous or surreal, even as he is deep into it." Trump, by contrast, is an example of what happens when extreme extroversion goes wrong: very little listening is taking place.

By reading this chapter, I hope that quieter teachers come to believe they have the capacity for successful leadership. If fear is keeping you from seeking more responsibility, remember the words of Nelson Mandela: "May your choices reflect your hopes, not your fears." Schools need more thoughtful, compassionate, quiet leaders who care genuinely about education. Too often, the cult of the individual has served to create schools led by fear, rather than trust.

I also hope for greater awareness of what quieter members of staff may be able to offer in leadership positions – these individuals could have a profound impact on their schools. Rather than discounting their potential, we need to support them to play a role that harnesses their talents.

In Part III of this book, we will step back into the classroom. We will turn our attention to the quiet and introspective skills that are absolutely essential if students – and their teachers – are to flourish.

A quiet reflection

Christopher Barnes (@MrBarnesTweets) has taught for almost 20 years in international and independent schools. For the past seven years he has been deputy head and head of prep at a non-selective 0-11 day school in Staffordshire. He was previously deputy head in the primary school of the British International School, Moscow.

Leadership found me more quickly than I could have anticipated. Half of my teaching career has taken place overseas, and in Russia, where I worked, promotions often happen quickly. At the end of my sixth year there, I was called to the general director's office to be told that I would be moving to one of the other parts of our (multi-site) school from September, as deputy head. That was all. No interview, handover or discussion. I felt very underprepared, only having been appointed as KS2 lead in the previous academic year.

Ten years later, and now in my second deputy headship, I am aware that being a quiet leader gives opportunities for misunderstandings, especially given the higher level of role visibility. Those who don't know you well can mistake quietness for aloofness, diffidence and a seemingly uncaring approach. Those who do see someone who is genuine, interested and reflective; pursuant of long-term and deep relationships rather than the shallow and quick-fix; an active listener and deeply engaged. They appreciate that a lack of small talk does not mean that you are disinterested but, rather, that you value opportunities to engage on a deeper level about fewer topics.

Interestingly, I found a reference from one of my former teachers that refers to this: "Christopher is a thinker and, as such, is not superficial with people, which may hint at a certain reserve. This is a mature characteristic, which must not be confused with a failure to relate to other people. Because of this reserve, he may be open to misunderstanding but those that know him well appreciate his fine qualities." Mrs Sadler knew me before I really knew myself; looking back on her words now, I can more fully appreciate them.

It took me a long time to become comfortable with being a quiet person, teacher and leader. In effect, there were two key events that helped me. One was a child whom I taught in Year 6 at my current school. She helped to demonstrate the power of quiet. In lessons, she rarely answered questions, but listened, absorbed, thought deeply and produced phenomenal work – and was also an amazing actor! The second confidence-builder came after reading Mary Myatt's *High Challenge, Low Threat* (specifically the chapter about "The Death of the Hero Leader"), *Quiet* by Susan Cain and *Quiet Impact: How to be a Successful Introvert* by Sylvia Loehken. They helped me to see that there is power in being a quiet person, which I had not previously appreciated.

As I enter my 20th year in teaching, I believe that it is crucial that children, parents and colleagues see greater links between quiet, calm and authority; that the cerebral, thoughtful leader is a person who has more impact on them than they realise. It is done in an unassuming way: the "reward" is in seeing that all has gone well, rather than anything overt. These people lead by enabling others to do their jobs well and therefore have greater input into the progress that is made by each child. It is therefore difficult to measure the impact of a quiet leader because what they do isn't always tangible – timetables, duty rotas, the daily running of the school, calendars, the logistics of special events – and yet their influence can be felt everywhere.

Introspection

1. Does your leadership style embrace quiet virtues and qualities?

2. Do you take the time in the busy school day to listen to other staff?

3. Do you demonstrate empathy and compassion in your leadership?

4. Is a calm and collected response to stress being modelled in your school?

5. What could you do to develop your potential as a leader?

PART III
QUIET AND
INTROSPECTIVE SKILLS

I think, therefore I am
René Descartes

CHAPTER 14
INTRINSIC MOTIVATION

When the reward is the activity itself –
deepening learning, delighting customers,
doing one's best – there are no shortcuts
Daniel H Pink, Drive: The Surprising Truth
About What Motivates Us

In the classroom, a teacher's attention can be consumed by what takes place on the surface: the behaviour of the students; the detail of our PowerPoint presentation; the classroom dialogue; and, most obviously, what we are asking students to do. Of course, these factors influence what happens in our lessons, but considering them alone amounts to a superficial assessment of learning.

What about the invisible web that supports genuine learning? The thinking processes, the emotions, the role of memory, the quality of the individual practice? We often overlook what is happening in our students' complex and still-forming brains: the social-emotional strategies that involve motivation, delayed gratification ("I'll do my revision before checking Instagram"), self-efficacy (the belief that they have the power to influence their own learning) and their ability or willingness to ask for help.

When I trained as a teacher, the Ofsted criteria for an "outstanding" lesson had "loud" written all over it: it had to be showy, collaborative and hurtle along at a "rapid pace". But a focus on these surface and external skills – the "noise" of learning – produces only minimal gains.

Instead, it is quiet skills – invisible and unseen qualities – that help young people to succeed. One of these, motivation, is particularly vital. When our students have it, we are delighted: they are engaged, driven and determined to do well; they learn with greater speed and more interest; they persist with challenging tasks, and work with curiosity and intensity. When they don't possess it, we are at a loss: they are apathetic at best and disruptive at worst.

Motivation, clearly, has a huge impact on the learning and engagement that take place in any classroom. The dynamics that influence it, however, are diverse and hard to control: peer relationships, previous experience of school, parental support, aspiration – the list is endless.

What is motivation?

The word "motivation" stems from the Latin for "move" (*movere*). When it was first used in a psychological context, in 1904, it was defined it as an "inner or social stimulus for an action". It is this focus on the internal that makes it particularly pertinent for this book.

My terrifyingly gigantic psychology reference text, *Psychology: The Science of Mind and Behaviour* by Richard Gross, has this to say on motivation: "Trying to define motivation is a little like trying to define psychology itself." Helpful. It then takes the reader on a mind-boggling journey from evolutionary theories of motivation to drive theories, attribution theories and collapsing-from-motivation-information-overload theories.

Regardless of its definition and complexity, motivation certainly fascinates us as an intellectual pursuit: how can we become more motivated? What does it take to motivate others? How can we break our procrastination habits and focus for long enough to achieve something worthwhile?

In this chapter, we will look at two different styles of motivation, and at how subtle changes to our teaching practice can boost students' motivation – or even switch it on.

Extrinsic v intrinsic

A search for books about motivation on amazon.com produces 50,000 results. For teachers, Daniel H Pink's *Drive: The Surprising Truth About What Motivates Us* is the needle in the motivational haystack. It is a brilliant synthesis of the research into motivation and defines our three key sources of motivation: a need for autonomy, a need to sustain learning and a need to have an impact on the world.

Pink argues that extrinsic motivation is driven by external factors such as money or praise. This type of motivation arises from forces outside the individual, as opposed to intrinsic motivation, which originates inside the individual. The distinction is important because the most obvious attempts made by teachers to motivate students are extrinsic. Just think of all those glittering motivational posters, those reward assemblies. The consequences of this, however, may not be as positive as we might think.

Extrinsic motivation

In schools, the most obvious form of extrinsic motivation is good examination or assessment results. I have been guilty of telling students as young as 11 that "this is the kind of question you will be expected to do once you reach GCSE level". This is hardly going to spur them into action, given that it will be five years before they reach that level. Too much focus on final outcomes means students have little appreciation of the value and joy of learning.

Praise and rewards are other common forms of extrinsic motivation. Praise is more complex and subtle: students do need positive reinforcement, but when praise is insincere or excessive, it can result in less effort. The more focused students become on short-term rewards, the less likely they are to sustain their effort over a longer period of time. The consequences of this can be a comparative mindset and a refusal to complete tasks unless a reward or a prize is on offer.

But it would be misguided to reject extrinsic motivation entirely, as highlighted by Marc Smith and Jonathan Firth in their book *Psychology in the Classroom: A Teacher's Guide to What Works*: "The promotion of extrinsic motivators has become common in school and educational settings, despite their negative consequences having been understood for some time. The basic idea is that students can be motivated by offering them an external, tangible reward ... The underlying assumption here is that most learning involves the study of material that is just too boring or undesirable to be able to develop a true passion for it, so the only way to engage students is to offer than a reward to do it. Extrinsic rewards can motivate, and when used well can be highly effective. At their worst, they can kill off any interest or passion that might have developed if the rewards were not offered."

Reward systems

On his blog, the English teacher Chris Curtis (@Xris32) presents a parent's view of the downsides of reward systems:

"I hate 'Star of the Week' with a passion. From my experience, it is rarely fair and it is often used to pander to the boys. Tom kicked a ball. Star. Peter ran a race. Star. The girls have to wait for their 'annual turn'. Yes, it often felt like a tick box exercise. Everybody would get a go once a year, because that is fair. It seemed to my daughters that the naughty boys got the award more often than them. The girls who wouldn't swear within fifty miles of a school would be overshadowed by the boys who have been known to swear openly. The girls could see what was going on. They worked hard and it was the naughty boys who got praised for something that was expected from girls. That made the one mention a year all that more important.

Popularity is an interesting thing. Most people want to be seen as being popular. However, I have seen how the 'popularity factor' has a damaging effect on girls. My daughters put themselves up for school council most years. They occasionally got it, because nobody else volunteered and the teachers selected the successful candidate. In the final year, the school made the decision a democratic decision and the school voted for school president. My daughters didn't get the role, because the school voted for the popular student in a fair and democratic process. The whole process was transparently about popularity and that was made public. The whole process became about highlighting how my daughters were not as popular as the other students.

The popular kids are usually the extroverts and the outspoken and confident students. I have sat through numerous school plays and assemblies listening to the popular kids and seen the other children hide in the sides, because they haven't got the confidence to say a line or two. School plays tend to draw attention to this. At times, I think we should rename school plays to 'The Popular Extrovert Show'. Not really a microcosm of schools, in my opinion. My daughters would love to have a bigger part, but they are not going to shout out for one. They are good."

Chris's words should generate much reflection about the use of extrinsic rewards: what about the quieter, more diligent students who go through their school careers unheralded by these systems?

Relationships and optimism

How can we go beyond superficial attempts at encouragement and inspire more complex forms of motivation? No research is needed to show that young people are more motivated in the presence of a teacher who is passionate, enthusiastic and can build positive relationships. As we have already learned, our interpersonal skills are hugely important in the classroom. The relationships we form are a big factor in how motivated students are in our subjects.

It is pure common sense: we all struggle to find motivation when our emotions are in a negative state. The fear instilled by my childhood maths teacher was, of course, a major reason for my lack of motivation in the subject. Dread, rather than enthusiasm, was the emotion I felt when walking towards that classroom door.

I remember that feeling, and how much it clouded my thinking, when I consider my own students. Teachers, after all, set the climate and attitude for learning in their classrooms. We overcomplicate many aspects of teaching, but genuine enthusiasm and a passion for our subject are two aspects that will help us to succeed in the classroom.

Autonomy and choice

In his book *Drive*, Pink argues that one of our most basic human needs is for autonomy and choice. This becomes more complex in a classroom environment: young people have no real choice about whether or not they attend school. The reality is that, when presented with options, often the choice they make is not the one that is best for them and their learning. Instead, it might be the easiest option, or the one they think they can be most creative with.

But there are ways in which we can offer students autonomy and choice in lessons, without generating hours of additional work for ourselves:

- **Activities**. Young people like to feel ownership and control over what they are doing – we all do. Introducing an element of choice to tasks can motivate students to invest more effort. This is not about making activities overly simplistic, but rather allowing some scope for students to influence the direction of the lesson. Choice can be combined with challenge – encouraging students to complete a task that is more demanding will help them to push themselves. The design of the tasks is key: they have to take young people forward in their learning.

- **Homework**. Homework can give teachers sleepless nights and consume a huge amount of time, in both the marking and the chasing. Giving students an element of choice in the homework activities they do can help to avoid the battles. Plus, more creative tasks that allow for engagement from students do not necessarily involve huge amounts of marking.

- **Projects**. Well-structured collaborative or independent projects offer a huge amount of autonomy – they allow students to delve into a subject and discover knowledge for themselves.

- **Relevance**. It is surprising how much more motivated students can be once they discover the relevance of what they are learning to their own lives. "Why is this important for your life?" can be a frequent discussion point in lessons. Such discussions can be much more powerful than vague references to exam results – young people can see that the hours they spend in class will have a meaningful impact on their lives. In my English lessons, I am forever going off on rants about the value of reading and about how literature can develop compassion, empathy and wisdom.

Academic success

We can have a long-term impact on motivation by changing students' perception of themselves as learners and by building self-efficacy. This cannot be realised through endless praise: we need to give students the opportunity to achieve real and genuine success in our subjects. Carl Hendrick and Robin Macpherson address this in their book *What Does This Look Like in the Classroom? Bridging the Gap Between Research and Practice*: "In thinking about how to motivate students it's probably more helpful to think about the kinds of things that will give students a sense of autonomy and mastery in the long term than the sense of inspiration in the short term."

Success needs to be balanced with challenge: students need to see that they can tackle and master more cognitively demanding tasks. This gives them visible evidence that they are growing and developing. So, how can we deliver lessons that provide this validation for our learners?

- Share the **design of the curriculum** with students. Present to them what they will be studying in individual sections of work; they can use this as a checklist, tracking the amount of content they are learning. For anyone, being able to track goals and progress is motivational.

- Break tasks into **manageable chunks** and reinforce achievement at each stage. This will scaffold success and build confidence among students. Using modelling and worked examples will make things even clearer for them.

- Encourage students to **set goals** for themselves that are achievable and realistic. These can be referred to regularly in order to focus their minds on what they need to do to improve.

- Regular **low-stakes testing** can boost motivation. This can be as simple as five questions to close a lesson, or ten recap questions to begin a lesson. Grappling with these will strengthen students' knowledge retention and show them the improvements they are making. Such testing will also make them more reflective, as they consider the areas they need to work on in more detail.

We also need to be judicious about when we remove the scaffolding and support from such learning. Too early and we may shatter the confidence students have developed; too late and they will become reliant on the scaffolding.

Better feedback

Motivation and feedback are, of course, completely interlinked. Feedback can help us to better understand our strengths and weaknesses, but if we are left to reflect on these alone, our introspection is likely to be influenced by a range of biases. As teachers know all too well, young people can completely overestimate their capacity to perform particular skills, and underestimate their ability in other areas. Expert guidance can help them to achieve genuine and objective insight.

The issue with feedback is that it is often delivered only through marking. The marking obsession can leave teachers stressed out and students overwhelmed. It can take up so much of our time as educators, so here are some ways that we can use its potential to motivate our students, without keeping us awake long into the night:

- **Create the conditions**. We need to show young people that feedback is vital in any discipline. Don't just throw their work back at them covered in red pen – help them to see the value in feedback by explaining that everyone needs to be open to it if they want to get better at what they do. We also have a responsibility to prepare them for less positive feedback – constructive criticism can help us all to develop and improve.

- **Verbal feedback**. When students are beavering away independently, I often find myself drifting around the room aimlessly. But this is the ideal time for teachers to guide, cajole and offer positive reinforcement. Face-to-face feedback is much more powerful than scribbling all over students' books. Keep a running list of the students you have spoken with, to make sure that they all receive your time and support.

- **Process-orientated feedback**. Reams of written feedback can disengage and demotivate students. Just one glance at mass of red pen can really knock their confidence – it is often a waste of your time. Instead, deliver selective comments that are clear, instructive and guide the student in their development. Even better is feedback that asks the learner to do something, to take active steps. This can be motivational: the student sees this as a dialogue, rather than an order. They can try again and see tangible improvement, and we get to witness the impact of our marking. Motivational for all!

- **Self-assessment**. Training our students in effective self- and peer-assessment can boost their motivation and help us to maintain some semblance of a work-life balance. Developing the capacity to accurately evaluate their peers' work can also help young people to feel more confident in their own abilities.

So, now that our students are remarkably motivated and engaged in our lessons (and we are significantly wealthier because we no longer have to buy chocolate prizes), we can turn our attention to another quiet skill. In the next chapter, we will consider how we can develop students' ability to focus.

A quiet reflection

Peps Mccrea (@PepsMccrea) is dean of learning design at Ambition Institute. He is the author of a range of books about education, including Memorable Teaching *and* Lean Lesson Planning.

At the time of writing this I'm just finishing off a book about how teachers can apply the "science of motivation" in the classroom. Despite a solid writing routine, I'm nearly a year past my original deadline. Richard Gross's proclamation rings hard in my ears – has it been a struggle because I've been trying to define psychology itself? Or perhaps even teaching itself?

While I very much doubt the answer is anywhere near yes in either case, the more I learn about motivation, the more central a position it appears to occupy in many of our daily pursuits. The trouble is, despite its ubiquity, I'm not convinced that we have a particularly clear or actionable definition of what motivation actually is or how it relates to learning.

Perhaps the most promising starting point for such a definition comes from thinking about motivation as the "allocation of attention". We triage the options available to us and invest our precious mental resources in the direction that we feel will bring us greatest returns. If we think this definition is useful, then the central questions around motivation become about "value". What we value is where our attention is allocated. What we attend to is what we learn.

As Jamie has suggested, the most valuable source of motivation in school is likely to be what Daniel H Pink would call "mastery", or perhaps, more crudely put, getting better at things. This is our main job as teachers, and so, to come full circle, our best chance of building enduring motivation is probably just to "first, teach well". As Jamie suggests, this includes things like breaking content down, pitching it appropriately, knowing your pupils and feeding back with care.

However, you will have no doubt spotted the circular error here! How can we get our pupils motivated to learn if the best motivation comes a result of learning? Indeed. This is where some of the other strategies that Jamie suggests come in handy, as a form of "bridge" toward mastery motivation. They include things like belonging, trust and a culture for learning in our classrooms. Again, this could easily be construed as "just good teaching". And so the driving question then becomes: how can I become a better teacher? Which will hopefully keep us motivated and attentive for quite some time to come…

Introspection

1. Do you rely on extrinsic motivation in your classroom and have you considered the impact of this?

2. Does your language communicate optimism and encouragement?

3. Do you provide options and choices in your lessons?

4. Can you build more autonomy and choice into homework tasks?

5. Do you link your lessons to young people's experience in the wider world and their futures?

6. Do you regularly celebrate your students' academic success?

7. Do you deliver frequent feedback in a variety of forms, not just written?

8. Can you train your students in effective peer-assessment?

CHAPTER 15
FOCUS AND THE
MULTITASKING MYTH

But amid the din and distraction of work life,
poor listening has become epidemic
Daniel Goleman,
Focus: The Hidden Driver of Excellence

There are three phrases that reverberate around any school: "pay attention", "now focus" and "I need everyone to listen". In no other profession are phrases such as these employed so liberally and often so ineffectually. Every teacher is painfully aware of how much energy, time and persistence they invest in trying to get their students to focus. They do this because focus is absolutely critical: without it, no learning can take place.

The issue of attention is, of course, one that educationalists have grappled with for centuries. The 19th-century philosopher William James wrote extensively about the role of attention in the classroom, long before the distractions became so pervasive. These words are from 1899: "The exercise of voluntary attention in the schoolroom must therefore be counted one of the most important points of training that take place there; and the first-rate teacher, by the keenness of the remoter interests which he is able to awaken, will provide abundant opportunities for its occurrence."

So, how do we get to the point where the constant repetition of those phrases is not so necessary? The next two chapters will offer an alternative perspective on how we might cultivate focus and listening in our classrooms.

The age of distraction

Are we living in an age of distraction? Alarmist newspaper headlines and cautionary tales of technology eroding our attention spans suggest that we are. There is no denying that 21st-century distractions are loud and addictive. Smartphones promise instant access to a seductive world that offers frequent feedback and gratification. Even adults find the online world alluring: apparently we check our phones every 12 minutes on average.

Thanks to my agonisingly slow and laboured writing process, completing this book required real focus. And in the final few months of writing it, I decided to move back to Scotland from England, change schools twice and train for a half-marathon. Meanwhile, my excellently named small child was hurtling towards the terrible twos and ruthlessly rejecting the naps during which I could previously steal a couple of hours of writing.

When I did manage to sit down to write, the distractions seemed ever more enticing. All too often I would drift into mindless procrastination, usually disguised as "online research". Thirty minutes would pass before I would realise that I hadn't written a thing.

If the online world has such power over adults, what is it doing to young people, who have even less capacity for self-control? What effect is constant distraction having on their ability to concentrate?

The multitasking trap

Some of our students are masters in the art of mind-wandering, so we need to work hard to make sure we don't provide opportunities for distraction. If a young person is not paying attention to the lesson, they will not be able to process new information and, in turn, transfer it to their long-term memory.

Multitasking is seen by many as the solution to productivity. Research, however, has shown that this is often not the case. More than anything else, multitasking results in attention that is split across a number of tasks, yet is not purposefully trained on anything.

In their book *The Science of Meditation: How to Change Your Brain, Mind and Body*, Daniel Goleman and Richard J Davidson tackle the concept of attention-switching: "Attention tasks don't really go on in parallel, as 'multitasking' implies; instead they demand rapid switching from one thing to the other. And following every such switch, when our attention returns to the original task, its strength has been appreciably diminished. It can take several minutes to ramp up once again to full concentration."

This is certainly true of my attempts to sit and write this book. Once I am distracted by another task (or rather, once I begin to procrastinate), my capacity to focus is diminished. When we do this attention-switching with our students, we see that it becomes more challenging for them to focus on just one thing. So, what can we do to create a learning environment that nurtures and supports concentration?

Mobile phones

Some people argue that mobile phones should be embedded into the curriculum and lessons, or that students should be allowed to have mobile phones in front of them in the classroom. My experience in a wide range of schools, with vastly different policies, suggests that this is naive at best and ignorant at worst.

Mobile phones are the principal object of distraction for most young people, so the first step in helping students to concentrate is to remove that object. Young people are often not aware of just how insidious the distraction is until it is taken away. Even knowing that their phone is in their pocket can affect their concentration levels. My first school had a zero-tolerance approach to phones; seeing the positive impact this had in a variety of ways has made me rather intolerant to liberal phone policies.

I may be opening myself up to charges of Ludditism, but I would argue that, much like adults, young people need a place of refuge from the technological world. Its addictive and competitive nature can be utterly exhausting. My father's school has just banned phones completely and he says that seeing young people engaged in conversation in the corridors is just one of the benefits of what is a challenging rule to enforce.

A few years ago, I joined a group of 17-year-olds on a charity school trip to India. We banned phones from the trip: we wanted the students to experience the joys of travelling and working in another country. Although at times it was difficult for them, they talked at length at the end of the trip about how much they enjoyed having some time away from their phones, and how this allowed them to better communicate with each other.

So, now we've banned phones from our classrooms, what else can we do to help our students focus?

Classroom environment

We have already explored the effect that an overly stimulating classroom environment can have on teachers' wellbeing. But as well as benefiting us, keeping displays to a minimum can also help our students to focus on their learning.

We need to be more judicious about when and how we share students' work. Step into any highly stimulating classroom and it is fascinating to watch what young people are doing when they are supposed to be learning. They look for as many distractions as they can – and classroom displays can be a tempting diversion.

Make sure that the displays you do have support their learning: for example, a "keywords" display can be a powerful literacy tool. Young people need frequent exposure to material and having a list of keywords on view can encourage them to use them in their work.

Behaviour

Behaviour is clearly a significant factor when it comes to the degree of focus in a classroom. This is why a quieter behaviour management style is so important: by addressing situations calmly, quietly and on a personal level, the whole class is not distracted.

It is the same with noise management: is the students' discussion and dialogue focused on the task in hand, or is it actually a distraction? In modern classrooms, noise levels are often such that children are unable to concentrate on any real cognitive demand.

Anxiety and stress

Anxiety levels can be significant in preventing the clear focus we need from students. In Daniel Levitin's book *The Organized Mind: Thinking Straight in the Age of Information Overload*, he highlights that "we attend to objects in the environment partly based on our will (we choose to pay attention to some things), partly based on an alert system that monitors our world for danger, and partly based on our brains' own vagaries". Our earlier examinations of the interpersonal factors that help students to feel comfortable are important here.

The clarity and calm of our teacherly dispositions can also be helpful: we need to reassure and reiterate that mistakes are a core part of any learning process. We need to communicate our expectations appropriately and, of course, avoid causing any unnecessary panic or stress. This is particularly important in the build-up to exams: we need to be aware that secondary students have a range of subjects to focus on and bear this in mind when setting expectations of how much work they do.

Passion and engagement

I may be accused of stating the obvious here, but students need to have some degree of interest in order to pay attention. We teachers cannot hope to gain their undivided attention if we are not enthused and passionate ourselves. Ask young people about why they find a subject boring, or less interesting, and often they list the teacher as a reason. There is a complex interplay between how the material is taught and the attention levels of those in the room.

It is a misconception that rigour and engagement cannot go hand in hand. Engagement is not about reducing our subjects to cheap tricks, but rather about building curiosity (more on that later). The reality is that dull, uninspired lessons lead to inattentive students and behavioural issues. Some aspects of our curriculum may be inherently less interesting than others, but it is our job to be cheerleaders for all facets of our subjects. We must never validate apathy by agreeing that a topic is dull.

As explored earlier, we need to channel our inner performer, even though this can be one of the most tiring parts of our job. At 8.25am (the start of the first teaching period in my current school), we will find lethargic young people. Their attention levels will remain low unless they are faced with positivity, energy and passion from us.

This does come with a disclaimer: how we move in the classroom can have a real impact on students' attention levels. I had a brilliant history teacher who paced the room manically while he talked, but stood utterly still when there was a key point or piece of information he wanted us to take away. There are positives and negatives to such an approach!

Emotion and curiosity

Appealing to students' emotions and natural curiosity is a great way to capture their attention. This is why is it so important to consider how we can make lessons relevant to their experience and age.

Emotion and learning are intimately connected, and learning becomes more memorable when it connects on a primitive and emotional level. When I was 16, Arthur Miller's play *Death of a Salesman* resonated powerfully with me. Willy Loman's attempts to be the best father he could, and the relationship between him and his brother, spoke to me in a way that no other literature had before. When it came to writing about the play, I was much more articulate and thoughtful because I had connected deeply with the human struggles at its core.

PowerPoint

The ubiquitous PowerPoint presentation may do more harm than good when it comes to securing students' attention. During our training year in particular they are things of beauty, enlivened by images, flashes and nifty changes. All this is done, of course, in the hope of engaging our students. But in reality, it splits attention heroically, with young people pausing to admire our delightful images rather than absorbing any of the information.

The vacant faces that young people adopt in the face of yet another PowerPoint presentation should also be a message to us all: sometimes we need to stop relying on PowerPoint to deliver material and try something different. Our own charisma and interpersonal skills can be much more meaningful and effective.

Cognitive overload

In lesson planning, it is important to design tasks with John Sweller's cognitive overload theory in mind. In very simple terms, we all have a limited cognitive capacity (the amount we can consider and retain), so it is essential that we do not introduce too much for our students to think about.

Not only do we need to minimise the cognitive demands on our students, but we also need to direct their mental efforts to where we really need them. Here are some ways to train their attention:

- **Modelling**. Instead of providing vague information about the output we are expecting from our students, modelling can help to prevent misunderstandings and sustain focus and clarity. In terms of eliciting passion and interest, a model that outlines what students could be capable of achieving is a great way to spark their competitive instincts.

- **Scaffolding**. Avoid overloading students by breaking down learning into key steps that get gradually more challenging. This will help to focus their thinking. The start of a lesson is when students are more attentive and switched on – if we can ensure focus at this point, it will be easier to sustain throughout the lesson.

- **Questioning**. One way to capture the attention of students is to ask questions – lots of questions. Questioning channels their thinking and forces them to engage with a concept. Rapid-fire rounds check the understanding of as many students as possible and encourage them to be attentive, thus aiding behaviour and focus.

- **Low-stakes testing**. Regular quizzes and moments of competition can boost attention. This can be done as a part of a routine – at the start of every lesson, for example. In no time, students will be eager to do well in the competitions and will be asking each other about previous material on the way to lessons. That's the hope, anyway!

- **Time**. Time is key to ensuring concentration. Breaking tasks up into shorter chunks of learning will help to maintain focus, and also allow time for feedback and reflection on the learning that is taking place. Timers show young people exactly how long they have on a task, which helps them to regulate their own concentration.

- **Stories**. There is a palpable change in atmosphere when a story begins in any classroom: young people are visibly interested and cannot help but lean in. Try to maximise the potential of stories in your lessons – most topics have a narrative that can be drawn out. If not, sharing the odd anecdote from our own wildly exciting lives can help to ensure attentive students. I tend to introduce creative or reflective writing with a short story I wrote about my experience of having all my clothes stolen from a student swimming pool while at university. A rather tight pair of silver Speedos may or may not have been involved.

Frequent feedback

We have already explored how feedback motivates and drives us to do better. All students need regular praise and guidance to keep them on-task and attentive. Make sure no one goes without by keeping a conversation checklist, marking the names of each student who has received feedback.

Sleep, sleep, sleep

One message that everyone involved in education needs to hammer home is how vital sleep is for young people. Issues with attention and concentration – and indeed stress and anxiety – are often the result of students sacrificing sleep for the numerous distractions that dominate their lives.

It doesn't take a genius to recognise that we pay less attention and absorb less information when we are tired. Teachers are not surrogate parents, but discussing healthy sleep patterns and encouraging good sleep hygiene will pay dividends, helping students to understand the impact of their sleep choices.

What should be our key messages around sleep? First, urge young people to put away all devices an hour before they go to bed (warnings of the blue electronic light zapping them awake should be delivered with hyperbolic zeal). Second, encourage consistency: going to bed and waking up at the same time, at least during the week. Finally, provide sound advice on the energy drinks and caffeine that drive lots of young people. An explanation of the crash effect and how long it takes for caffeine to leave the bloodstream might make them think twice before they devour yet another can of the delightfully named Monster.

It is difficult to overestimate the importance of the discussions we have explored in this chapter. Without the ability to focus and pay genuine attention, no young person is going to thrive in the professional world – or gain the examination grades they need to get there. Yet the nature of our society means that attention is more fragmented than ever.

Our job as teachers becomes even more challenging in this dynamic – we have to find new ways to cultivate concentration. This often means providing a break from the clamour of instant messaging and the internet. To end on a note of optimism: most young people are desperate for this space to think and – importantly, for our next chapter – this can help them learn to listen intently.

A quiet reflection

Mark Enser (@EnserMark) is head of geography and research lead at Heathfield Community College in East Sussex. He is the author of Teach Like Nobody's Watching *and* Making Every Geography Lesson Count, *and is a regular TES columnist.*

When I started teaching, I gave pupil attention a lot less thought than I do now. It was reading Daniel Willingham's book *Why Don't Students Like School?* and stumbling upon his maxim "memory is the residue of thought" that changed my approach. I now spend much longer considering what my pupils will be thinking about and where their attention will be.

In the past I thought more about the activity that pupils would be doing. If I wanted them to learn about the factors affecting the risks posed by a natural disaster, I might have asked them to use their own research to create a newspaper front page about that disaster. Their attention here, though, would be on anything but the thing I wanted them to learn. They would be thinking about how best to search for the information they needed, they'd be thinking about the layout of the newspaper front page, the title of their newspaper, even what price to put on it. The lack of attention paid to something they had to think hard about often meant the room was noisy, as pupils were busy but unfocused.

Now, I try to think more about where their attention is directed: what will they be thinking about? If I want them paying attention to the factors affecting the risks posed by a natural disaster, then I need to give them high-quality information about a natural disaster and show them why risks were created. I need to draw their attention to salient points through questioning and use this to link different ideas together. This focus on attention has also led to the need for a calm and studious atmosphere in the room, so that people can think hard about the questions I pose and so that they can think about and respond to the points people raise.

Thinking about where my pupil's attention will be, rather than simply what they will be *doing*, is now one of my main concerns as a teacher.

Introspection

1. Are you falling for the multitasking myth?

2. Could your own productivity improve with a more disciplined approach?

3. Does your environment cultivate concentration among students?

4. Could your teacher dialogue and explanation be more focused to ensure students retain information?

5. Do you consider the issue of cognitive overload when you are preparing lessons?

6. Do you plan moments that engage or inspire curiosity in students?

7. Are you falling into the PowerPoint repetitive-delivery trap?

CHAPTER 16
DEVELOPING
LISTENING SKILLS

Most people do not listen with the intent to understand: they listen with the intent to reply
Stephen R Covey

In this age of rapid communication, the art of listening is sadly neglected. We find ourselves in an increasingly bombastic world in which shouting the loudest seems to be the way to gain the most attention. This helps to feed a narcissism that is as far from listening – and from seeking to understand other viewpoints – as you can possibly get.

It is refreshing to spend time in the company of someone who does listen intently; someone who gives us the space and time to articulate ourselves, and does so without judgement. This skill embodies the quiet values we have explored in this book. There is no doubt that good listeners develop a better understanding of situations and of people – and this, in turn, gives them the ability to respond more effectively.

Professionally, listening is a vital skill in any organisation. It is, of course, the bedrock of all effective communication and understanding. If the two core aims of schools are to prepare young people for the workforce and to help produce well-rounded, interpersonally confident adults, then they should undoubtedly endeavour to teach the skill of listening.

Why listen?
Classrooms place extensive listening demands on young people. So extensive, in fact, that the challenge of sustained listening is often a source of significant conflict and behavioural issues.

Young people are not only asked to listen to ensure comprehension and learning, but also to ensure they understand instructions and to assess the quality of their peers' answers. Anyone who has spent time in a classroom will be aware that this process does not happen by magic: listening is an active process that is decision-dependent. It is therefore worth having frequent conversations about listening and taking the time to train students to listen well.

Be a role model

To encourage our students to be good listeners, we need to act as role models. There is no point in berating their inattention if we are not effective and respectful listeners ourselves. However, it is challenging for teachers to listen intently in the classroom. We face a wide range of distractions: managing behaviour; the content of the lesson; the epic to-do list we need to tackle afterwards; the million and one things in our lives outside school that, of course, we cannot completely switch off from.

Mindfulness and meditation can, as explored earlier, help us to be more present in our classrooms. If we can train ourselves to be less focused on our internal thoughts, we can be more in tune with and listen more carefully to the young people in front of us. This is necessary for classroom relationships to thrive.

For the self-esteem of our students and for them to feel comfortable sharing ideas, they need to feel that we are being attentive. So, what are the basics of the listening skills we want to model to our students? Some are verbal and some are non-verbal.

Non-verbal

- **Eye contact**. Listening and eye contact are completely interlinked. It can be challenging to sustain eye contact with a student who is speaking, as we need to scan the classroom to see how their peers are responding. But it is important to make as much eye contact as possible: it signals respect, attention and care. Your students must maintain eye contact with the speaker, too: respond to any interruption or chatter with exaggerated shock and horror, exclaiming, "In this room we look at people when they are talking and respect that they are speaking – we are not rude!" Alternatively, return to the earlier points about kindness, explaining that listening to one another is a way of showing kindness and respect.

- **Body language**. Try leaning in and displaying open and attentive body language when a young person is speaking. This non-verbal encouragement helps to boost their confidence, as they recognise your interest and see they are being given the space to contribute.

- **Smile**. In any discussion about the extent to which teachers should smile, it is important to consider what our teaching would be like without warmth and compassion. Ultimately, we would be robotic, cold and dispassionate – not qualities that would encourage or motivate our students. A listening smile shows engagement, allowing students to see that they are appreciated. Mirroring their facial expressions, to demonstrate appropriate concern or other emotions, will show that you are connecting with what they are saying.

- **Pause.** The temptation, as explored earlier, is to jump in quickly at the end of student dialogue and offer our own judgements. But leaving a few seconds once a young person has finished talking gives them time to offer more detail, or to allow the rest of the class to reflect on what has been said. Space and time will help all students to become more thoughtful communicators.

Verbal

- **Praise.** It is very easy to slip into insincere praise when we want to encourage students to feel confident and offer more. Genuine and specific praise, however, can achieve both of these aims. A considered comment such as "I like how you have…" will prove far more effective than "Fantastic answer" or something similarly vague. Young people are savvy: they know when we have not genuinely engaged with what they have said. Picking out keywords from their answer or elaborating on their points shows them and the whole class that this is a place where people are heard and respected.

- **Summarising.** Ideally, we want students to listen intently and follow a conversation to the end. Paraphrasing or summarising a dialogue can help to maintain their attention: "This has been a really interesting discussion. Let's recap on the three main points." Once we have modelled this, we can ask students to try it: "I will be asking one person to summarise this conversation in five minutes, so make sure you listen carefully."

- **Questioning.** There is nothing better than when students start questioning each other, asking for a summary or clarification of what has been said. This is a skill that we can model and is also a very simple means of differentiation: "Can you say more about…", "Can you go back to that earlier point and provide me with some more detail?" Since entering the world of podcasting, I do this more and more in my lessons – often in a cheesy chat-show style!

Listening ladder

As the leader of the classroom, our actions set the tone, atmosphere and value placed on listening, but there are ways for us to encourage students to take ownership. School 21, an all-through school in London, uses a fascinating method called the "listening ladder". The listening ladder sets out the various listening skills and ranks them in order of complexity; it can be used to help students reflect and set targets for improvement. The higher up the ladder a student goes, the more sophisticated their listening skills are. These are the rungs on the listening ladder:

- Summarising the speaker's ideas.

- Asking questions that dig deeper.

- Asking questions to clarify understanding.

- Reacting and refocusing.

- Offering nods or short words of encouragement.

- Giving eye contact to the speaker.

- Being calm and still.

- Giving 100% of your focus to the person speaking.

Open-ended questioning

While school ethos can make a real difference, there are practical classroom strategies that we can use to encourage listening. One simple approach is frequent open-ended questioning.

In classrooms where questioning occurs with intense frequency, the quality of listening quickly improves. Students learn that they cannot switch off when discussions take place, as they may be asked to respond to the points raised. This helps to sustain focus and maintain good behaviour.

Write it

Inevitably, there will be some students who do not engage – either cognitively or verbally – with the question that has been posed. As discussed earlier, we need to make sure all students contribute, including those who find it hard to speak in front of their peers. Asking students to draft an answer in their book, on a Post-it note or on a mini-whiteboard that they can hold up as feedback, means everyone engages with the discussion and considers a response.

Assigning roles

For younger students, assigning roles that they must perform during lessons can be a good way to develop listening skills. For example, the responsibility of the jazzily named Word Detective is to write down impressive vocabulary that has been used in the lesson and feed back on it later. Swap the roles around during the lesson so more students get the chance to do this.

Listening challenges

Short, quick listening challenges can be a good way to build a classroom culture that values listening. I often do this when I read a poem to a class. I read it slowly and deliberately, but first I tell the students that I will expect them to write down afterwards as much of the poem as they can remember. This switches them on to what I'm saying and helps them to focus on the quality of the language – an important feature of an English student!

At many points in this book I have considered how much we let superfluous noise and activity dominate our lessons. But, of course, I recognise that communication is necessary in any classroom context. Real communication, however, cannot take place without listening. Work on developing your students' capacity to listen with intent and you will reap the rewards.

A quiet reflection

Doug Lemov (@Doug_Lemov), the author of Teach Like a Champion, *places listening skills at the heart of teaching and learning. In this article, originally published by TES and reproduced with the kind permission of Doug and TES, he outlines five steps to improve the quality of classroom listening.*

1. Get students writing

Writing is a key part of the solution. In fact, it is the single most important tool for discussion – a statement that might sound counter-intuitive. Getting students to write responses to a discussion question means every person involved will have an answer. This, of course, holds everyone accountable to respond. After all, some pupils need to speak up a little more in discussions. But some need to speak up a little less. Writing lets you manage the difference.

The power of writing to shape discussion goes even further. Because it is permanent, it can be a record of change over time.

So, imagine doing the following in your classroom: pose a question for discussion and ask every student to write an answer to the question. Now everyone is prepared. Seek out a strong and reflective response and ask the student to share it, to kick off the discussion. You can then circulate and encourage some students to weigh in because the response they wrote will further the discussion. That's great for you and great to help them understand when their ideas are especially useful to share.

But the real value comes after the discussion, because the best post-discussion activity you can do is to say: "Now go back to your original response and revise it [or answer it again] based on the discussion we've just had." In doing that, you have changed the purpose of the discussion. Where once the implicit goal might have been to win it – to be the person who was right all along – now your students' goal is to find ideas they can use to develop and change their thinking.

If the question was about evaluating Napoleon's decision to attack at Waterloo, perhaps they will have gleaned additional information to cite. If the question was about social justice, perhaps they might now use the perspective of someone else to revise their first thought.

As they do so, they create and make permanent for themselves and for you, the teacher, a record of that change. In fact, if you wanted, you could even double down on this post-discussion. You could say, "OK, before we wrap up, I'd like to hear how some of you changed your opinions", or even better, "Which comments from your peers most influenced you?"

This question gives an opportunity for public praise of the comments that students were most able to connect with, and thereby those that most influenced the perspectives of others. I suspect it won't usually be the comments of the shouters that are chosen.

2. You should be writing, too

Consider the problem of remembering what others have said. Cognitive scientists often point out that we are all prisoners of short-term memory – we can keep precious little in our heads at any given time. Within a few seconds of engaging a thought, we begin to forget it. Striving to keep it in our working memory makes us unable to think and listen to other ideas. First, we forget who said it and their exact phrasing. Soon the idea itself is gone.

Unless you are charting, that is. Charting is writing down shorthand versions of key points on the board during discussion. This keeps them alive. As the teacher, I can glance at the board and recall the gist of what Chris or Christina said. I can refer back to it, build off it, develop it. Students can do the same.

It may sound simplistic, but one reason participants in large discussions don't build off – and refer to – one another's ideas is that they cannot remember them fully or retain them in short-term memory while thinking of their own idea. Charting helps overcome that and builds a strong incentive to respond to, and engage with, the ideas of others in the room.

Of course, it's even better if students are charting, too. Not only does this teach them to take notes, but it socialises them to listen for – and expect – value in what their peers say. Some of the best teachers I know at leading discussion always make sure students have place and time to take notes on what their peers have said.

3. Create response habits

Another useful tool for encouraging listening is "habits of discussion". This involves helping students to practise using phrases during discussion that help them build off one another, such as "I'd like to develop Marcus' point that…" or "I hear you, Andrea, but I also think there's another way to interpret that quote".

This is critical to giving pupils an alternative to seeing the world as my-way-or-the-highway. It's a replacement behaviour for arguing simplistically.

4. Introduce tracking

This one is a bit controversial: tracking – the idea of making it a habit to "track the speaker". That is, to turn and look at them while they are talking. One of the things that happens when students track the speaker is they say with their body language, "I am listening. Your ideas matter."

Neither you nor I would make honest or intellectually risky comments in a meeting if we did not feel those same sentiments from our peers. Students are not much different. Tracking helps students feel like their words will be respected. But what's more, it helps student listeners pay attention. They learn what it means to be attentive, to actively listen.

5. Make the aim clear

Again, this is a simple but important point. When you engage a discussion question, make it specific and write it on the board. This offers a constant and subtle reminder of the topic. For example, our discussion is not just an opportunity to say any old thing we want to say about this chapter in *The Giver* – we are discussing whether Jonas' father is morally culpable for his role in "releasing" children.

This allows us to stay on topic. If you get a comment that's unproductively off topic, you can simply point to the topic and say, "Thanks for that, but let's try to stay a bit more focused on this question." Or you could steer the discussion in more productive directions by saying something such as, "Remember the question hinges on the word 'culpable'," and perhaps then underline that word to help students focus on it for a sustained period of time.

By keeping your students focused on a collective purpose, you send the message that we are working together to come to an understanding of an idea. We are not just all of us expressing ourselves. We are engaged in shared inquiry.

Of course, it's unfair to say that our classrooms are responsible for the fractious times we live in. But it's also unfair to our students not to acknowledge the ways in which our classrooms might make things better. What we communicate about discussions, while we are having them, is a great way to start that process.

Introspection

1. Do you explore the importance of listening with your students?

2. Do you model the skill of respectful listening?

3. How often are students encouraged to demonstrate active listening and offer feedback?

4. Could you include listening challenges in lessons?

5. Could you use writing challenges to strengthen and develop listening skills?

CHAPTER 17
THE ROLE OF
INDEPENDENT PRACTICE

Practice is the single most important factor in determining a person's ultimate achievement in a given domain
Anders Ericsson and Robert Pool, *Peak: Secrets from the New Science of Expertise*

Clichés abound on the role of practice: practice makes perfect; practise and you will achieve your dreams. It is a narrative that speaks to our hopes for our own future potential – work hard on something and you can be the best. Fuel was added to the fire when Malcolm Gladwell, in his book *Outliers*, popularised the idea that 10,000 hours of practice will lead to expertise.

The research of the psychologist Anders Ericsson was the basis for Gladwell's rule. But what Gladwell ignored was that the complexities of practice cannot be boiled down to a random number of hours. In a 2012 paper called "The Danger of Delegating Education to Journalists", Ericsson wrote: "The 10,000 hour rule was invented by Malcolm Gladwell ... who stated that 'researchers have settled on what they believe is the magic number for true expertise: ten thousand hours.' Gladwell cited our research on expert musicians as a stimulus for his provocative generalization to a magical number."

I'm fairly sure that my childhood and adolescence involved well over 10,000 hours of football, and to date my career high has been staring (or surviving) in central midfield for Carrbridge FC in the Highland Welfare league. Alex Ferguson never called.

On its own, repetitive practice is not enough. Something much more subtle and precise needs to take place. The question that teachers should be asking, as facilitators of a significant amount of practice in its various forms, is what *kind* of practice has a meaningful impact?

Exit the comfort zone

In the rush to build collaboration and discussion into lessons, we often neglect an essential part of the learning process: the opportunity for students to practise independently. We have taught them some of our hard-won knowledge, we have discussed and unpicked it as a class, and there might have been some (carefully structured) independent dialogue about it. But the students haven't yet grappled alone with the processes that have been explored. We might think they have grasped the knowledge, but this is merely guesswork.

The real test of a student's understanding is, of course, the work they complete individually. This is why it can be so depressing when we mark their work and see the misconceptions they have picked up from a lesson that we thought had walked them faultlessly through some tricky concepts.

In their book *Peak: Secrets from the New Science of Expertise*, Anders Ericsson and Robert Pool provide some clarity on how students can become more expert learners. Their conclusions have significant implications for what we ask students to practise and how they complete their individual practice. A key consideration is the level of challenge. Consider these words from *Peak*: "This is a fundamental truth about any sort of practice: If you never push yourself beyond your comfort zone, you will never improve."

This was one reason why Alex Ferguson never came knocking at my door (the other was my lack of footballing talent!). I completed many hours of slavish practice in my garden, but usually I merely attempted to re-enact the epic goals scored by whoever was the prevailing footballer of the day. Neither did I receive a huge amount of feedback – my elder brother's criticisms of my lack of passing didn't achieve a huge amount.

Ericsson is a proponent of *deliberate* practice and he has identified feedback as a key feature of this: "One of the main criteria is for the classroom to be set up in such a way that students can repeatedly perform tasks and get immediate feedback in an individualised way. Hence, if a student is just listening to a teacher with everyone else, lecture style, or listening to other students solve a problem, this does not meet the criteria for deliberate practice."

Repetition equals retention

How do we know that students have really grasped something? Well, they might be able to perform a skill or task straight after it has been taught to them. That is why it is important to follow the delivery of lesson content with immediate practice: it allows us to circulate and see how much our students have understood. This gives us a chance to correct any misconceptions or, even better, help students to recognise where they might have gone wrong.

There is a clear difference, however, between the short-term and long-term acquisition of knowledge. We need students to grapple with the same material much more often than might seem necessary, in order to help it transfer to their long-term memories. According to the book *Make It Stick: The Science of Successful Learning* by Peter C Brown et al, "The striving, failure, problem solving, and renewed attempts that characterize deliberate practice build the new knowledge, physiological adaptations, and complex mental models required to attain ever higher levels."

So, repetition equals retention. The frequent revisiting of key concepts needs to be an important part of what happens in our classrooms, as highlighted in *Make It Stick*: "Repeated effortful recall or practice helps integrate learning into mental models."

What to practise?

This is where things become more complex and nuanced. Practice needs to be broken down and scaffolded, in order to ensure that it is useful for students. There is no point in asking students to work on material that is too vague or overarching – we need to define the component steps. Once we have done this, we can start to remove the scaffolding and support so that students gain the ability to work independently.

In her book *Making Good Progress? The Future of Assessment for Learning*, Daisy Christodoulou writes:

"Whilst skills such as literacy, numeracy, problem solving and critical thinking are still the end point of education, this does not mean that pupils always need to be practising such skills in their final format. Instead, the role of the teacher and indeed, the various parts of the education system, should be to break down such skills into their component parts, and to teach those instead.

This means that lessons may look very different from the final skill they are hoping to instil. For example, a lesson which aims to teach pupils reading may involve pupils learning letter-sound correspondences. A lesson with the ultimate aim of teaching pupils to solve maths problems may involve them memorising their times tables. The idea here is that the best way to develop skills does not always look like the skill itself."

It is crucial that we rationalise such an approach, explaining to young people that by practising simpler skills or learning smaller chunks of knowledge, they can develop more complex skills or larger bodies of knowledge. They need to be able to see the strategic purpose of what they are doing.

Five stages of deliberate practice

The maths teacher Craig Barton, in his book *How I Wish I'd Taught Maths,* breaks deliberate practice down into five steps:

1. Isolate the skill.

2. Develop the skill.

3. Assess the skill.

4. Final performance.

5. Practise again later, so the skill is not forgotten.

Let's explore these in depth.

1. Isolate the skill

Our first step is very important: we need be crystal clear on what skill we want students to practise. This will provide them with very specific goals to work towards. We need to be reflective and dispassionate about our subjects, making sure we are not falling into the various traps that come under the banner "the curse of knowledge". This describes a cognitive bias by which, because of our expert status, teachers are oblivious to the difficulties that novice learners may experience in their subjects.

Steven Pinker, in his book *The Sense of Style: The Thinking Person's Guide to Writing in the 21st Century,* highlights the impact of this: "The better you know something, the less you remember about how hard it was to learn. The curse of knowledge is the single best explanation I know of why good people write bad prose."

It is a sobering thought for us as educators: have we considered the true extent of what we are asking young people to do? In my own subject, I previously felt that I gave students lots of opportunities to practise – their books were full of writing. Yet I was demanding far too much of them; I was asking them to complete tasks that were too complex and vague. Rather than unpicking what makes effective descriptive writing, for example, I would show an engaging image and ask students to write a paragraph of description.

These days, I try to break down the writing process into concrete steps. *The Writing Revolution: A Guide to Advancing Thinking Through Writing in All*

Subjects and Grades, by Judith C Hochman and Natalie Wexler, is full of routines that "break the writing process down into manageable chunks and then [have] students practice the chunks they need, repeatedly, while also learning content".

As Doug Lemov writes in the foreword to *The Writing Revolution*: "Merely repeating an activity is insufficient to get you better at it ... for practice to improve skills, it has to have a specific and focused goal and must gradually link together a series of smaller goals to created linked skills ... deliberate practice requires all-in focus, and that is maximized in a short and intense burst."

2. Develop the skill

This is when we get students to focus on honing a specific skill. For example, in my descriptive-writing mission, I now spend time explicitly teaching the concept of figurative language. Students then have time to practise this specific skill before we seek to build figurative language into the more complex task of descriptive writing.

3. Assess the skill

Are we confident that students can now perform the skill confidently? We might use the end of the lesson to question them on their understanding, or try a low-stakes quiz to test their knowledge.

4. The final performance

This is the culmination of the deliberate practice. Students should complete this part of the process with no support or notes, merely their own understanding of what has been covered.

5. Practise again later

As Barton writes in his book, "Successful performance at the assessment stage may not be a reliable indication of learning." We need to return to the material periodically, reviewing the key aspects that students may have forgotten. This will help to secure the material in their long-term memories.

How much practice?

I would argue that at least one section of every lesson should involve some sort of independent and deliberate practice. We need to make sure this quiet time is seen as celebratory, not punitive, by our students: it is their opportunity to prove to themselves, and to us, that they are learning and developing.

Another way to justify independent practice to students is by referring to the research of the psychologist Mihaly Csikszentmihalyi, in particular his book *Flow: The Psychology of Happiness.* Csikszentmihalyi's "flow" refers to the conditions in which we find ourselves immersed in a task – your goal or outcome is clear and you must use your skills to overcome a challenge.

Csikszentmihalyi writes: "Contrary to what we usually believe, moments like these, the best moments in our lives, are not the passive, receptive, relaxing times – although such experiences can also be enjoyable, if we have worked hard to attain them. The best moments usually occur when a person's body or mind is stretched to its limits in a voluntary effort to accomplish something difficult and worthwhile."

It is interesting to consider Csikszentmihalyi's concept of flow in relation to our earlier explorations of intrinsic motivation. He has said that the highest intrinsic motivation is a flow state where self-consciousness is lost, one surrenders completely to the moment and time means nothing.

Deep focus

Ideally, deliberate practice should involve short, intense bursts of quiet concentration. According to Ericsson, "Engaging in deliberate practice requires full concentration, which cannot be sustained for [an unlimited] time per day, especially for students in lower grades. The ideal school day must therefore be a combination of different types of learning activity, where deliberate practice can be only a fraction of a six-hour school day."

While students are engaged in their quiet practice, we can circulate, providing verbal or written feedback as appropriate and underlining the importance of acquiring this particular skill.

As this chapter has made clear, repetitive practice on its own is not enough. Students should receive feedback, but they should also be trained in how to evaluate their own work. I played golf obsessively when I was a teenager: one summer holiday I played almost every day for six weeks. All this practice, however, didn't make a huge amount of difference to my performance – my drive still swerved bizarrely and I couldn't putt to save my life. Something was missing: I didn't know how to effectively evaluate my own game. We will look at this piece of the puzzle in the next chapter.

A quiet reflection

Zoe Enser (@GreeboRunner) is specialist subject advisor for English with The Education People base in Kent. This blog was initially published on teachreal.wordpress.com

Let me take you back to the summer of 1970-something. It was my seventh summer and, much to my parent's growing frustration, I was still inexplicably unable to ride my bike without stabilisers. They had tried everything: lifting the training wheels up or removing one stabiliser to encourage me to balance more by myself; telling me to watch someone do it; firmly instructing me to try harder; and moaning at me every time they saw me wobbling away on my little purple shopper. They even tried a complicated mechanism whereby I had to try cycling between two fixed planks to keep my wheel upright, and I won't even go into the story of the "Well, let's just see what happens if we push her down a hill" day.

I'm not writing this to paint a picture of my parents as monsters. They weren't, and I can understand their frustration – my older brother had achieved this with seemingly little effort. They themselves could barely remember the moment they leapt from two legs to two wheels. I, it would appear, was stuck. I couldn't grasp the independence they wanted me to have, which meant I continued to wobble around the garden in clumsy circles, as opposed to whizzing along a lane with joyful abandon. I was still too dependent and that simply wouldn't do.

The desire for 'independent learners'

Recently, I have been having a lot of conversations with teachers about dependence and independence. Lack of independence seems to be the bane of many teacher's lives and, much like my parents, it seems to lead to much frustration and soul-searching. This is the one thing many of the teachers I speak to would want to change in their students. They long for them to throw off those training wheels and fly. It seems like the holy grail of teaching, where we see happy and engaged students embarking on complex tasks with little, or no, input from us. But why is it still not happening and what is it we are trying to achieve? Do we expect to see independence in every lesson? Should it be at the end of a teaching unit? How on earth do we get them there?

To return to my bike-riding memories, I think there were a number of things which delayed my independence. First, I only had my older brother to demonstrate the process. My "model" was eight years older, four feet taller and sitting atop a racer! I could see little relation between myself and him.

Secondly, I rarely got to practise. Even though I was lucky enough to be bestowed with a size-appropriate bike each time I outgrew the last one, for at least eight months of the year it sat in the shed. When it was dragged out from behind the various broken bits of car and gardening equipment, it often had at least one flat tyre and dodgy brakes. Another month might pass before said beastie was in full working order, and then the practising could begin. Very slowly. Very much like I had never sat on a bike before. The much-needed muscle power in my legs had been depleted and the first half an hour was simply spent trying to get the thing going without needing a push.

Finally, when the support was being dismantled, it was happening much too quickly – after all, the summer was rapidly disappearing and the bike needed to be packed away. I still hadn't mastered the skills I needed for balance, though, and I didn't have the strength. My tentative attempts were met with frustration, both from myself and from my increasingly disappointed parents. I wanted to whizz down the road with the wind in my hair but I frequently landed flat on my back, sometimes with quite painful consequences.

Building to independence in the classroom

I can see a number of parallels between my experience then and that of my students. Like many of my students, the model I was given needed to be broken down to be within my reach. I needed to understand the steps that it took to get to the dizzying heights of my older brother (he could even ride without holding on to the handlebars!), and while it was good to know what the finished product might look like, it was completely unattainable for me at that stage. I am a huge advocate of using high-quality and aspirational models in my classroom, but these need to be carefully selected for the class and used as models, not just examples. I use a lot of live modelling to demonstrate my processes, illustrating each step and allowing students to explore the stages as we go. That might include me modelling a simple opening sentence and students then taking that further, or it might mean me modelling more extensively, but explicitly telling the students what I want to achieve and how I am aiming to do this.

Students need the chance to practise each step carefully; therefore, I get them practising different parts of the process, sometimes allowing them to focus on finding quotations, sometimes on analysing individual word choices, sometimes on writing about the big ideas in a text.

Once they are ready, I will begin to remove the supports I have put in place. This is a delicate moment, which may be at very different points for different students, different classes and different tasks. If they are removed too quickly then the student could come clattering down and find it too difficult to get back up; some students may have fallen so many times they simply don't bother any more. It's also safer to stay down as it is not so far to fall next time. The timing here is crucial and should be informed by knowing where your students are at. I make sure I monitor the class very closely at this stage, too, quick to add a keyword or sentence to the board, or to give a verbal reminder. If necessary, I will work with a small group in the class to continue to support them, while the rest of the class get on with their practice more independently.

Once they have had these opportunities, they can become more fluent in that particular activity and may then be able to move to complete independence. We can sit back and watch as they enjoy the ride. But it is important to be mindful that if the context, complexity or parameters of the task change radically, then the supports need to be put back in until they are ready to be withdrawn again. After all, you have just put them on a different bike. Possibly on a hill. Maybe with some bumpy bits. They will need some guidance to get used to it again.

Culture and the problems with transfer

My own cycling experience also came back to me when reading Adharanand Finn's book *Running with the Kenyans*. It was interesting to note that there has been a distinct difficulty in transferring the athletic prowess of Kenyans, so renowned as distance runners, to cycling. Kenyan runners dominate in the world of distance running, so the cycling coach Nicholas Leong selected a group of men who demonstrated both power and speed, with the view to transfer those skills to a bike. As you will note from the lack of Kenyan cyclists competing in the Tour de France, this was not successful. Roads in Kenya provide effective surfaces for runners, less so for bikes. Running is regarded as an efficient, cheap mode of transport for most of the community, including children; bikes, in contrast, are expensive and cumbersome. Kenyan athletes are immersed in a culture of running, surrounded by people at top-level as well as everyday runners. They have neither the inclination nor facilities to become cyclists, even when a world-class coach from Singapore turns up waving a shiny new bike.

It is therefore apparent that, like myself and the Kenyans, my students need to be provided with the right conditions, equipment and opportunities to practise their skills before independence can occur. Some students may already have had exposure to this environment, an environment where they have been immersed in books and reading for pleasure, exposed to culturally rich dialogues filled with history, music and art, and given opportunities to experience a myriad of different viewpoints. These students will not only know what a bike is, but will have seen a range of different models, learnt about its history, seen others riding it and know about the experience. Others might not have even seen a bike.

It is this last group of students who I think we really need to be aware of when seeking independence. Independence is, of course, a desirable aim for all, but will it always be something that can be achieved at the end of a lesson, the end of a unit or the end of a year? Some will be able to achieve independence at different times and we need to provide them with what they need en route to achieving this. If there is one thing my early cycling experience has taught me, though, it is that in our quest for independence, we must be careful we don't just push our students down the hill and hope they start pedalling. Let them keep the stabilisers a while longer, give them a push when needed and don't feel too bad if they are still wobbling too much. Independence is an end goal, not a starting point.

Introspection

1.   Do you give your students regular opportunities to practise?

2.   Do you break their practice down into chunks?

3.   Do your students understand that they are taking part in a long-term learning journey?

4.   Do you create the conditions for deliberate practice to take place?

CHAPTER 18 METACOGNITION: OWNERSHIP AND REFLECTION

Thinking: the talking of the soul with itself
Plato

Metacognition is arguably the most complex of the quiet skills evaluated in this section of the book. It promises to change our students forever and, in turn, save us huge amounts of time. Its proponents declare that they have "no need for hours of marking! My students are metacognitive wizards – they seamlessly identify all their mistakes and self-correct!" They argue that metacognition is the holy grail when it comes to developing independent learners.

Despite such glowing testimonies, an unknown proportion of teachers shift uncomfortably in their seats when metacognition is mentioned. The term is certainly becoming more commonly used, but are we really sure what metacognition means and what it can deliver in schools?

What is metacognition?

A common misconception is that metacognition is simply about the process of thinking. That's a fair assumption to make, but it ignores the word's "meta" prefix, which can be defined as showing or suggesting an explicit awareness of itself or oneself as a member of its category. So, metacognition is about more than merely the act of thinking. Instead, it refers to the process of thinking about our thinking.

This idea was first labelled "metacognition" in 1976, when the American developmental psychologist John Flavell defined it as a state of heightened awareness of one's thoughts processes: "Knowledge concerning one's own metacognitive processes or anything related to them."

Before this, the Soviet psychologist Lev Vygotsky (1896–1934) had developed the idea of the zone of proximal development. This involves the complex interplay between what a learner can achieve independently and what they can do with the guidance of an expert. Initially, it is the expert (in our case, the teacher) who leads the process of learning: setting goals, monitoring progress, planning and considering where attention needs to be paid. The result of this scaffolding should be that responsibility is ultimately transferred to the learner. Their increased ability to regulate their own learning is the aim of metacognitive development.

My gigantic psychology reference book, *Psychology: The Science of Mind and Behaviour* by Richard Gross, provides a helpful clarification of exactly what we are dealing with here: "Performance on a whole range of tasks will be better if the child can monitor its own performance, and recognise when a particular strategy is required or not. This self-monitoring improves fairly rapidly, beginning at school age."

This will prompt understandable scepticism from teachers who have sat through generic "learning to learn" lessons with students, which seem to make very little difference to their ability to become more effective learners.

The utopian vision of students accurately monitoring their own progress, and improving their capacity for self-assessment, is challenging to achieve. Anyone with experience of working with young people is aware that some lack the capacity to discern their level of understanding. While some students have misplaced levels of confidence, others wildly underestimate where they are at.

Jonathan Firth, whose "quiet reflection" you will find at the close of this chapter, expands on the reasons for this in his book *How to Learn: Effective Study and Revision Methods for Any Course*. He writes: "Our metacognitive beliefs about our own learning and knowledge can be flawed. Many people think they know what is working for them in terms of study, but these judgements tend to be based on a perception of how easy it feels, and how quickly they are making progress."

Self-assessment or peer assessment can be an opportunity for misconceptions to be reinforced, and often deny young people honest and useful feedback. There is always a glorious disconnect between the "Fantastic – I love this!" and what has actually been produced. So, how can we help students to gain a more realistic and meaningful understanding of their ability level?

Our subjects

The first thing to note is that when we are training our students in metacognition, we need to do so through our subjects. One-off interventions or lessons on thinking skills are likely to prove ineffectual and will be quickly forgotten.

We also need to remember that our students are novices and the "curse of knowledge" means we are likely to underestimate the difficulty of our subjects. To boost our students' chances of metacognitive success, we need to take a clear and dispassionate look at our subjects and work out where the traps might be.

Repetition

We want our students to have such a strong grasp of metacognitive strategies that they become automatic when they are working independently. The more we practise metacognitive strategies, the more likely this will be.

A phrase that I may patent for its pure beauty is "make classrooms metacognitively open". Embedding metacognitive practices in lessons will ensure that students see their benefits and use them in their own work. Frequent practice, however, must be accompanied by evaluation. For example, students should be prompted to judge the effectiveness of their learning method by considering past performance.

Planning

Planning is something that most students neglect completely, but metacognition starts before students tackle a piece of work. We want them to slow down and first think about how they want to approach a task. This, of course, requires careful consideration of their prior knowledge and learning.

As an English teacher, I despair when students dive straight into a piece of writing without any sense of direction. To teach planning well and help students to become independent planners, we can try strategies such as teacher modelling, diagramming, practice, answer checking, checklists and goal attainment. We can encourage students to ask themselves the following questions as they consider a task:

- What task have you completed recently that has been similar to this?

- What are the skills you need to perform this task well?

- What have been your strengths and weaknesses in this kind of task previously?

Modelling

A 2018 report published by the Education Endowment Foundation, entitled *Metacognition and Self-Regulated Learning*, said that an effective way to strengthen students' metacognitive skills was actively modelling the processes: "Modelling by the teacher is a cornerstone of effective teaching; revealing the thought processes of an expert learner helps to develop pupils' metacognitive skills."

This involves walking students through each step of the process that we ultimately want them to be able to do independently. Modelling provides students with an insight into our expert thinking and encourages them to mirror our strategies. Live modelling takes confidence, but it can have a real impact: students gain clarity on what they need to do and how they can do it. There is nothing wrong with scripting your modelling before you demonstrate it to students – this would be a much more meaningful investment of time than creating yet another PowerPoint display!

Phil Naylor, assistant director of the Blackpool Research School, has written on the school's blog about how he uses modelling in his science lessons: "I personally use an iPad/Apple pencil and Apple TV combination to work through examination questions in front of the class. I model the way to tackle the question and the strategies I am trying and how I know if they are successful. I will take live feedback and monitor how successful the approach is and as a class we discuss and adapt."

It is important to be honest about the stumbling blocks that students might encounter, and explain to them how they can conquer these challenges in the learning process. By talking about our own difficulties and sharing with students the strategies we use to overcome obstacles, we can humanise learning for them. Perseverance is key – students need to understand that it is tenacity, not some innate talent, that will get them over the hurdles.

Practice

In the previous chapter, we explored how deliberate practice needs to be broken down into its component parts and scaffolded for students, before the scaffolding is gradually removed to prepare them to work independently. An analysis of the research on metacognitive teaching strategies, by Arthur K Ellis et al, highlights the importance of guided and independent practice:

"Whether students speak, write, or illustrate their thinking, practice is a critical element. Effective practice is both guided and independent. Guided practice means that the teacher orchestrates student use of the strategy through examples, demonstrations, and feedback. Having students imitate the teacher's use of the strategy is also appropriate when students are first exposed to the strategy. Independent practice is assigned once students demonstrate sufficient mastery. Whatever product students create as a result of independent practice also receives teacher feedback and is used to check student understanding."

Reflection

Instead of just completing a task and switching off, reflection is the final stage in the metacognitive cycle. We can use it to encourage students to take ownership of their work once it is completed, and to help them become more aware of their strengths and weaknesses.

Again, we are responsible for training them to do this. We need to build in time for evaluation at the end of the independent practice stage. We also need to insist that work should not be handed to us without the student first considering its success. It might be helpful for students to have the opportunity to talk about their work with others before they reflect on it independently. If they can also compare their work with a teacher model, they will have extended their knowledge of exactly how to perform the task.

All these strategies encourage students to take ownership of their work, allowing them to grow and develop in confidence as independent learners. Rather than didactically spoon-feeding them all they need to know, we can use these quiet and introspective processes to prepare them for the thinking they will need to do in their professional lives.

That brings us to our next exploration: in any job they hold in the future, young people will need to demonstrate creativity. Can we – and should we – try to develop that in our classrooms?

A quiet reflection

Jonathan Firth (@JW_Firth) is a psychology teacher, teacher educator, author and researcher. After teaching secondary school psychology for many years, he now works in teacher education at the University of Strathclyde. He is the author of a range of books about education, including The Teacher's Guide to Research *and* How to Learn.

Metacognition can be difficult to define, with the result that different teachers may end up talking at cross purposes when they try to discuss its uses and benefits.

In simple terms, metacognition relates to many strategies that are already widely used by pupils, and generally considered to be helpful by staff. Examples include planning out longer answers, checking for and correcting errors as you work on a task, and reflecting on your own performance after completing a piece of work. More broadly, any strategy that involves thinking about a learning process can be considered metacognitive, whether this happens before, during or after the learning process itself.

Although these things are already being done in most classrooms, there is a strong argument for doing them more often and more effectively. When I was a new teacher, it was fashionable to run "thinking skills" classes, sometimes scheduled in registration/form time or as part of PSHE. However, this kind of generic approach to metacognition can be very hard for pupils to apply in practice.

I would therefore agree that we are often better to teach such strategies within normal class time and in a way that is directly linked to topic content. This can include using terminology with our learners, making it easier for them to discuss metacognitive strategies with us (for example when planning their work or revision) and among themselves (Pintrich, 2002).

Practising such strategies in class will help learners to start using them in their own independent study and revision, too. However, when working independently, learners are often misled by a sense of ease – they assume that if something feels easy then it must be working well. In reality, strategies that make short-term performance easier are often less beneficial for durable learning (Soderstrom and Bjork, 2015). For example, skim-reading a textbook chapter is both easier and less effective than testing yourself on the material. As a result, learners often stick to ineffective revision habits such as highlighting notes or flicking through slides on a screen, even when better alternatives have been demonstrated to them in school.

How can this problem be tackled? I have personally found that giving a clear and evidence-based explanation of how learning works has often helped to make a breakthrough. This can include summarising psychology research studies which have directly compared two or more strategies. My pupils who were preparing for exams have been interested and often very surprised to find out that so many popular revision strategies are actually ineffective!

The latter point also applies to teachers; even experienced teachers do not always recognise that current performance (such as getting answers right repeatedly in class) can be short-lived, because forgetting is rapid.

So while quiet professional reflection is certainly to be encouraged, it is more likely to be effective if it is based on a thoughtful reading of the research literature on areas such as metacognition and self-directed learning. Fortunately, this information can be accessed in an easily digested form through things like the Education Endowment Foundation's 2018 report on metacognition, or the many accessible books and articles that tackle the issue – including this book.

Introspection

1. Are you clear on what metacognition involves and its benefits?

2. Do you model and talk about all aspects of the learning process with your students?

3. Do you help students to develop the skills to plan effectively?

4. Can you introduce monitoring points in lessons to help students track their progress in independent work?

5. Can you build in time to allow students to reflect on their work after it is completed?

CHAPTER 19
SPACE FOR CREATIVITY

Imagination is more important than knowledge. Knowledge is limited to all we know and understand, while imagination embraces the entire world and all there ever will be to know and understand
Albert Einstein

Creativity has been somewhat neglected in the educational limelight recently. Its intangible nature makes it difficult to quantify in terms of classroom practice, and it seems out of place in the world of assessment and data. It has also come under fire from traditionalists, who argue that the knowledge curriculum should be at the heart of everything young people do in schools.

Sir Ken Robinson, perhaps the most ardent defender of creativity in schools, has argued that modern education kills young people's natural creativity. In his famous 2006 TED talk, "Do Schools Kill Creativity?", which has now been viewed more than 60 million times, he offers this stark warning: "My contention is all kids have tremendous talents. And we squander them, pretty ruthlessly. So, I want to talk about education and I want to talk about creativity. My contention is that creativity now is as important in education as literacy, and we should treat it with the same status."

Although I certainly wouldn't endorse all of Robinson's points, the fact that his talk has resonated with so many people suggests this is a discussion that cannot be ignored. However, for teachers with full timetables, creativity seems somewhat whimsical. With the ever-increasing pressures that teachers are under, it can often be the first thing that is lost in planning.

The rigorous changes to modern specifications only push it further down the list of teacher priorities: how do we find time for creativity when we have so much curriculum content to get through? Added to this is the fear of losing control: the risk that a more creative task will result in a classroom of wild children erupting into a *Lord of the Flies*-style rebellion.

In this chapter, we will put creativity under the microscope. Is it still relevant and important in modern society? And what position, if any, should it have in schools?

What is creativity?

To define creativity is a significant challenge in itself. Let's go back to the words of Ken Robinson: "You can be creative in math, science, music, dance, cuisine, teaching, running a family, or engineering. Because creativity is a process of having original ideas that have value. A big part of being creative is looking for new ways of doing things within whatever activity you're involved in. If you're a creative chef, for example, then your originality is going to be judged in terms of cuisine. There's no point applying the criteria of modern jazz to somebody who's trying to create a new soufflé."

What does that mean for us in the classroom? This definition of creativity implies that we should be encouraging original and unique approaches, certainly not curtailing our students' enthusiasm with prescriptive ways of working.

Creativity in schools

It may seem extreme, but perhaps it is useful to consider what the educational world would be like if it were devoid of creativity. What would life be like for students in schools that didn't allow them to use their imagination, express their individuality or be inventive? Indeed, what would society be like if we all followed the same conveyor belt of expectation?

One adjective springs to mind: dull. If we do not seek to inspire creativity and originality, we risk producing young people who struggle to think for themselves; young people who are homogeneous, identikit, clones of one another.

Learning can and should be joyful – full of laughter and full of creativity. It would be a sad state of affairs if our teaching was solely focused on assessment objectives and examination criteria. Children and adolescents need a certain degree of creativity, fun and engagement. Young people are often far too liberal in their use of the word "boring", and although teachers do not exist to entertain them, we want to encourage creative thinking that does require some degree of novelty.

In his book *Creativity: The Work and Lives of 91 Eminent People*, the psychologist Mihaly Csikszentmihalyi (who identified the concept of "flow") wrote: "Of all human activities, creativity comes closest to providing the fulfillment we all hope to get in our lives."

Creativity, then, makes life more interesting and reminds us of its many possibilities. It is also, in part, about the voyage of self-discovery. Let's return to the wisdom of the writer and neurologist Oliver Sacks: "For better or for worse, we are all created uniquely different and we have to find different ways of doing things creatively."

So, how can we foster creativity in our students? And how do we encourage the innovation that will take society forward? First, it is interesting to consider how lessons might be structured to enable moments of creativity.

Lesson starters

We need to establish the conditions and ethos of creativity in our classrooms. The start of a lesson is a fertile opportunity for students to be creative and can set the tone for the rest of the lesson. We might present an interesting image, or some kind of conundrum that students have to solve. By feeding their imaginations right away, we indicate that the rest of the lesson will seek to challenge and extend their thinking.

Creative questioning

Part of the role of questioning is to inspire original thought. Often, though, we merely ask process questions or fall back into the "guess what is in the teacher's head" trap. Questioning can be fun and joyous, and young people love the opportunity to think in a different way.

The close of lessons can be a time to embrace more creative styles of questioning that encourage students to think conceptually. When unpicking the motivation and dynamic of a literary character, I often like to make students consider bizarre-seeming questions and then justify their answers. Here are some of the questions I use:

- If Lady Macbeth was a chocolate bar, what would she be and why?

- If Atticus was a hot beverage, which would he be and why?

- Which piece of fruit would this poem represent and why?

- If Lennie was a breakfast cereal, what would he be and why?

Another way to stretch our students' thinking is to get them to ask questions themselves. Young children do this all the time – they endlessly interrogate what is happening around them. Somehow, by the time they reach adolescence, much of that questioning spirit has been lost.

Establishing questioning points in lessons can be a good way to encourage this innate curiosity, even if you just use the trusty Post-it notes and ask students to write down any questions they might have about the lesson so far. We can model this ourselves, by musing on questions that start "why", "how" and "what if".

Making connections

Part of the creative process is making interesting and novel connections between different things. We want our students to search for trends and patterns in the lesson content and in their experiences, reinterpreting and applying their learning in new contexts. One way to get them to think more conceptually is to ask them to connect a topic to other aspects of their learning, and to justify the reasons for those links.

Visual learning

Images can provide great inspiration for creative and exploratory thinking. Picture prompts can work for all kinds of tasks, helping to make connections between different aspects of learning and to encourage empathy with characters. I often use the atmospheric paintings of Edward Hopper to inspire creative writing and characterisation, asking students to reflect carefully on the situations that the artist depicted.

YouTube clips have a huge amount of potential in the classroom – for example, you can ask students to find links between a clip and the unit of work they are studying. Clips also break up lessons, allowing for moments of more visual learning.

Creative freedom

In my first school, I was asked to redesign the key stage 3 curriculum with the English department. We decided to teach a poetry unit that had creativity at its heart. The concept was that each poem was introduced with a launch lesson to enthuse students about its content. This involved conceptual explorations of the poems themselves – for example, a poem about homelessness was introduced with a classroom set up as a homeless shelter.

Students were given a journal at the start of the term, and the homework task for the half-term break was to come up with their own interpretation of the poem in their journal. This was, in part, inspired by the journals of Leonardo da Vinci, who filled more than 7,000 notebook pages with questions, doodles, observations, sketches and calculations. Some of the more artistic English teachers (definitely not me!) modelled journal interpretations of the poems.

By the end of the term, some of the students had produced amazing journals packed full of wonderfully creative ideas. Equally important was the fact that they had really engaged with the concepts presented in the poems. For me, this experience confirmed that creativity can help young people to connect with ideas and meanings. It can help them to make stronger memories of their learning, and the choice and autonomy that come with more creative tasks can boost motivation and provide a sense of ownership.

Problem-solving

Structuring a lesson around a problem is another way to make classrooms more creative. Thomas Tallis School in London takes a particularly interesting approach to problem-solving, known as "extended learning enquiries".

This is how the approach is described on the school website: "Assignments that are genuinely open ended require students to wonder, question, explore and investigate. However, such investigations need to be supported in various ways. For example, there should be some sense of a minimum expectation, a simple guide, a clear timescale and possibly even a great example. Extended Learning Enquiries, at their best, can inspire amazing levels of engagement, pride and excitement. But if they're not well designed, they can lead to mediocre work and very little learning."

Such tasks need to be carefully planned and scaffolded to enable creativity, and we also need to tread carefully if the enquiries involve group work. As we have seen in earlier chapters, group work is often a context in which extroverts dominate and the voices of introverts go unheard. Teachers need to balance group work with time for individual exploration and contributions.

This chapter posed the question: is creativity still important in modern education? Without doubt, it needs to feature in every teacher's repertoire – classrooms should be places of awe, wonder and joy. Of course, this would be impossible to achieve in every lesson, but if we have gone for weeks without doing something different and dynamic, then perhaps we are not connecting with our students' need to be enthused by the process of learning. A lesson that stands out for its distinctive nature may make a student think deeply, help them to remember an aspect of their learning, or encourage them to produce original and provocative work.

We all need a degree of creativity in our lives, otherwise we become jaded and uninspired. Put energy and dynamism into the work you do with young people and the chances are that they will give you energy and dynamism back.

A quiet reflection

Dave Grimmett (@daveg5478) is head of English at Churchill Academy in North Somerset. He runs the teaching and learning blog tlideasblog. wordpress.com

In my early teaching career, in the now much maligned 2005–10 era, I once delivered a lesson on writing about the senses for my little Year 7s. For smell, I put some fir cones and some flowers in a bag, and invited a student to take a whiff and describe what the smell conjured up. The class wrote down with interest what he announced: the woods and flowers. For hearing, I asked them to close their eyes and write down what they heard and felt as I put some audio of a stormy night on. They added to their notes: wind, loneliness, rain against the windows. Finally, for sight, I asked one student to open the door (unbeknownst to them I had bribed at break time three sixth-formers to burst in on cue with crazy masks and mock swords and jump on the tables).

What did those students remember from that lesson? The madness of it all. Did they remember any specific strategies for writing about the senses? Probably not in that *particular* lesson.

Did they write some of the most imaginative work in that lesson, and the lesson after, that I had seen that year? Yes, they did.

Four years later, when I spoke to the lovely girl whom I gave the chance to open the door, did her eyes light up at the memory of that lesson? Yes.

Seven years later, this was the moving message I received from that same girl: "Just wanted to send a quick message to thank you for the genuinely incredible job you did teaching me in Year 7. I'm in my last year of sixth form now and am going on to do art in college but I don't think my love for English would have survived this long if you hadn't made it as engaging as you did in those first years."

Don't get me wrong, I'm a huge convert to traditionalism, but I'm not a 10/10 one. I have shaped my department's vision towards embedding learning over time, use retrieval quizzes in most lessons, have built in interleaved weeks, have knowledge organisers coming out of my ears, and ensure every student who comes into an English classroom is au fait with the Learning Scientists' (@AceThatTest) work about effective retention strategies. I know you actually can't begin to be "creative" without the prerequisite knowledge in your locker. I've read *Make it Stick, Memorable*

Teaching, Why Don't Students Like School? and all the seminal edu-works of recent years; they've blown me away.

But, and it's a big but, I've been increasingly uncomfortable lately with the mocking of the concept of fun and engagement; with the way many edu-tweeters dismiss many creative lesson efforts as ludicrous and an utter waste of time.

However, as an aspiring senior leader, I can see many of the arts heads of faculty glazing over when I talk passionately about the knowledge agenda. If we are to get some of these people to 3/10 traditionalist, we need to not lose sight of their world.

There is absolutely a way that *knowledge and fun* can co-exist in this brave pseudo-Dickensian new world...

Where's the harm in asking your students to try and imagine themselves in a war zone for ten minutes? (Yes, yes, I know, if they haven't got adequate prerequisite knowledge of a war zone, they'll struggle, but still, let them have a go! Empathy is a core value we should seek to nurture every day.)

What's the problem with taking 15 minutes to insert your students' names and their interests into a grammar activity to make it that little bit more "fun"?

To follow some silent poetry analysis skills practice, let's give students the opportunity to create a poster that amalgamates some of the main images and keywords from a poem. Hey, that's a schema right there, isn't it?

Let's continue to create our own amusing acrostics to help us remember persuasive techniques in the upcoming assessment. Let's dedicate some time to confident speaking in our public speaking unit, and give students choice to talk about anything they want, even fun stuff like "Why Justin Bieber should not be allowed to sing on this planet". I want our students to be able to write well, but I also want them to deliver with aplomb, and if that takes up a couple of weeks just focusing on hand gestures, eye contact and dramatic pauses, so be it. I wish I could dedicate more time to catching up those public schools that do it so well.

Don't be afraid to take two lessons out to get students acting out the plot of texts with some props. We've had a lot of fun with this over the years, and students always remember the lines they delivered in front of the class!

I love the way our "knowledge organiser" homework learning tasks are open to creative interpretation, and that students can do funny little artistic things with them to help them learn.

Our knowledge organiser starter recap quizzes actually get a cheer, as the students love the fun competitive element I have introduced. Those five or six students who achieve the highest scores each time earn rewards, and believe me, it's not always the same people or the highest attainers who earn those rewards.

We give over two lessons at the end of a module to creating inventive board games to recap knowledge from the previous term. Students came in at break time to finish these – they were so keen to get them just right. The creative pride was tangible and the fun they had playing them was wonderful to see.

As I draw to a close, I think about my own children who are aged four and six. Do I want some liberal provision where they get to choose whatever activity they think is the most fun? No, that's utterly misguided in my view. I want them led to practise hard in all areas of the curriculum. But, do I want them now and again to come home with their eyes full of excitement regaling me with the Tudor battle they re-enacted, or the 3D model of Mars they've admirably created out of a plastic yoghurt cup? Do I want that buzz to continue into secondary school? Damn right I do. 10/10 traditionalists forget we learn through emotion too:

"Things that create an emotional reaction will be better remembered" – *Daniel T Willingham*

To conclude, then, of course we should get our students to engage in deliberate practice. We should ensure our lessons use all the evidence-based components that point to progress: modelling, recapping, interleaving, silent reflection time, whole-class instruction. But we sure as hell should ensure they smile now and again, and laugh now and again, and compete now and again, and are creative now and again, and say "Hey, that was pretty fun" now and again, because if they don't, I might as well be back in my bloody office job doing dull administration every day.

Introspection

1. Have you got the right balance between rigour and creativity?

2. Is there scope for some creative freedom in your lessons?

3. Could your students complete an open-ended creative project?

4. Could you use images to make connections between lesson content?

5. What kind of problem-solving activities could you try in the classroom?

CHAPTER 20
COMPASSION AND EMPATHY IN THE CLASSROOM

If you can learn a simple trick, Scout, you'll get along a lot better with all kinds of folks. You never really understand a person until you consider things from his point of view ... until you climb into his skin and walk around in it
Harper Lee, To Kill a Mockingbird

In 2006, when Barack Obama was a US senator for Illinois, he was asked to give a commencement address at Northwestern University. In advance of his visit, a student, Elaine Meyer, wrote an article for the school newspaper entitled "Challenge Us, Senator Obama". With the characteristic modesty of youth, she outlined exactly what she expected from Obama's speech: "It shouldn't hurt us to be challenged for 30 minutes, especially on a day that marks our commencement into the 'real' world."

Obama responded directly to Meyer's demands, posing some challenging questions to the young adults about the kind of life they wanted to lead and the values they should prioritise. And he offered this as his "first lesson of growing up": "The world doesn't just revolve around you. There's a lot of talk in this country about the federal deficit. But I think we should talk more about our empathy deficit – the ability to put ourselves in someone else's shoes; to see the world through those who are different from us – the child who's hungry, the laid-off steelworker, the immigrant woman cleaning your dorm room."

This idea of an "empathy deficit" was a constant in Obama's political career: he delivered frequent and urgent reminders of the need to "put ourselves in someone else's shoes". In 2013, when he was president of his country, he returned to this theme in a commencement address at Morehouse College, a historically black men's college in Atlanta, Georgia:

> "And I will tell you, Class of 2013, whatever success I have achieved, whatever positions of leadership I have held have depended less on Ivy League degrees or SAT scores or GPAs, and have instead been due to that sense of connection and empathy – the special obligation I felt, as a black man like you, to help those who need it most, people who didn't have the opportunities that I had, because there but for the grace of God, go I. I might have been in their shoes. I might have been in prison. I might have been unemployed. I might not have been able to support a family. And that motivates me. So, it's up to you to widen your circle of concern – to care about justice for everybody, white, black and brown. Everybody."

Obama's eloquent call to "widen our circle of concern" resonates so powerfully because, politically and personally, it stands in such direct contrast to today's prevailing values. We are constantly fed a message that our core purpose is to be "successful": to be rich, famous, entertained. The narcissism and conflict so central to social media have, if anything, made this lack of empathy even more pronounced in the years since Obama responded to Elaine Meyer's call. The way in which we access news can also lead to compassion fatigue – we read and hear of so much suffering that we are unable to genuinely empathise with the experience of others.

In this divided and competitive world, how can we teach our young people about compassion and empathy? They spend a significant proportion of their formative years in our classrooms, so we are partly responsible for making sure they grow up with a strong understanding of the complexity of human existence and experience.

Essential empathy

First and foremost, empathy-rich classrooms help students to develop the self-awareness and ability to form relationships. In his seminal book *Emotional Intelligence: Why It Can Matter More Than IQ*, Daniel Goleman suggests: "If your emotional abilities aren't in hand, if you don't have self-awareness, if you are not able to manage your distressing emotions, if you can't have empathy and have effective relationships, then no matter how smart you are, you are not going to get very far."

This is a key message for young people, particularly given the mental health pressures they face. In the modern secondary school in particular, so much emphasis is placed on academic achievement that we neglect the development of emotional literacy and resilience. When young people enter the workforce, their capacity to build relationships and work with other people will often be more important than whatever glittering academic achievements they have. Their ability to manage their emotions – to cope with the stress and demands of the modern workplace – will also be hugely important.

Empathy and compassion, therefore, are essential for young people to thrive. We also need them to be prepared to offer opinions and challenge oppression and hatred, and a keener sense of empathy can help them to do this. Much like academic intelligence, however, empathy and compassion are not fixed. There is much we can do to develop these qualities.

Positive relationships

The word "empathy" is inspired by the German term *Einfühlung*, meaning "feeling into". To create empathy-rich classrooms, we first need to focus on "feeling into" relationships.

I make no apology for repeating this throughout this book: classrooms are interpersonally complex environments, and part of our responsibility is to make these environments as respectful and compassionate as we can. No matter how young or old the students are, we need to teach them that respect, care and compassion should be foremost in all interactions. All the minor and major exchanges we have with our students carry emotional messages and influence how they will respond to us in the future.

Powerful and transformative moments can arise when we recognise – and celebrate – that a student has displayed empathy and acted in care and concern for another. Modelling empathy ourselves – with the calm, kind demeanour that we have discussed throughout this book – will help students to learn that every interaction should be humane and careful.

Showing emotion

I fully comply with most stereotypes of an English teacher and I often feel real emotion when discussing a work of literature with my students. It is important to be open and transparent about these emotions. In their book *Boys Don't Try? Rethinking Masculinity in Schools*, Matt Pinkett and Mark Roberts call this "militant tenderness". Pinkett has written on his teaching blog about how he models emotion in the classroom:

> "Whilst I would never discuss my personal life in any depth, I will openly discuss the feelings and emotions that arise in the context of what's being

studied or discussed in the classroom. If a poem makes me very sad, I'll tell the class. If a kid makes me look at something in a new and exciting way, I'll express my childish delight. And, if a kid does a piece of work that's absolutely mind-blowing, to the point where it makes my heart swell with pride, and my eyes with tears, I'll acknowledge that fact, frankly and openly. In fact, I'll intentionally draw the class's attention to it. I'll say: 'That's making me well up with pride, that', and face them, smiling and watery eyed."

If we show that emotion is a healthy and important part of life, we free our students up to show their feelings, too. Offering appropriate insights into your emotional life will help to cultivate your empathy-rich classroom.

Empathy in every lesson

Every subject offers opportunities for the discussion of empathy, but doing this effectively requires sensitivity and care. We need to encourage our students to identify with other people's perspectives. Here are some questions we can ask to help them:

- How would you respond if you were in that situation?

- What's it like to be in that person's shoes?

- How do you think they feel at this moment?

Of course, some subjects and some aspects of subjects better lend themselves to discussions about empathy. It may be harder to find these opportunities in maths lessons than in English lessons, but they can indeed be found!

The power of reading

As the former children's laureate Malorie Blackman has said, "Reading is an exercise in empathy; an exercise in walking in someone else's shoes for a while." This is one of the reasons why it is so important to promote reading in all subjects – it helps young people to find meaning and to look beyond themselves.

Let's return to the words of Barack Obama. In a conversation with the author Marilynne Robinson, published by *The New York Review of Books*, Obama said: "The most important set of understandings that I bring to that position of citizen, the most important stuff I've learned, I think I've learned from novels. It has to do with empathy. It has to do with being comfortable with the notion that the world is complicated and full of grays, but there's still truth there to be found, and that you have to strive for that and work with that. And the notion that it's possible to connect with some[one] else even though they're very different from you."

This is not merely a theory – extensive research has been carried out into the powerful impact of reading on our empathy levels. In a report entitled *Exploring the Link Between Reading Fiction and Empathy: Ruling Out Individual Differences and Examining Outcomes*, Raymond Mar et al found: "Readers of fiction tend to have better abilities of empathy and theory of mind."

In his book *The Empathy Instinct: How to Create a More Civil Society*, Peter Bazalgette writes that "arts and culture, by their very essence, tell us stories about the human condition and help us to understand and live with our fellow citizens". According to Bazalgette, neuroscientists have shown that when we see people in pain, the neurons in our own brains "fire in the same way as if we ourselves were in pain". He says we have "the ability to imagine a fictional person is in pain, and still empathise" and concludes that "when we tell and listen to stories, we rehearse our human responses".

Aidan Severs, the primary school deputy headteacher who provided the "quiet reflection" at the end of chapter 4, has written about the importance of developing empathy in schools:

> "Children, for many reasons (one biological one being that humans tend to display tribal behaviour by default), don't always deal with differences in a kind and empathetic manner. It makes it more difficult for them when all around them there are examples of intolerant adults committing atrocities as a result of their inability to understand others.
>
> A school's RE curriculum is vital when it comes to learning about one of the most divisive aspects of humanity: religion. Much of the PSCHE curriculum seeks to engender a better understanding of others. Indeed, a lot of what goes on in schools in general is to do with the social aspect of getting along with one another. But often these important subjects get squeezed out of the curriculum, often because subjects for which schools are held accountable are given the most prominence.
>
> But, hang on! What is one of those subjects? Reading! Yes! And we must capitalise on this – children can learn all they need to know about religion, culture, nationality, sexual orientation, identity and so on from the books that they read during those reading lessons and all that time spent reading at home ...

... We teachers are not just teaching children to read so they can enjoy themselves, find things out or get a job; we are teaching them to read so that they can change themselves and the world. We are teaching them to read so that they understand the issues facing them as they grow up in a world full of differences – differences which books can teach them to celebrate."

We can open up important conversations by giving young people the chance to share with each other what they are reading – and, importantly, what they have learned as a result.

Compassion in assembly

There is something almost church-like about a school assembly: the rows of attendees, the hushed silence, the reverence for the speaker. Tradition dictates that this is how assemblies usually function, and thus their potential to deliver messages is profound. In my masquerade as a school leader, this was one of the few areas where I felt I could deliver something effective.

At that school, assemblies involved a 30-minute speech. Each one had me fretting for weeks in advance, but the introverted preparer in me made sure that I knew exactly what I was going to deliver. The way I saw it, this was my classroom but on a much larger scale. And as with my teaching, I wanted empathy to be central to my messages.

I delivered one assembly on the theme of compassion, based on the song *Skinny Love* by Bon Iver: "And I told you to be patient/And I told you to be fine/And I told you to be balanced/And I told you to be kind." I explored a range of case studies that demonstrated compassion and care for others, and concluded with a video from the Blind Trust Project. In the video, a man stands on a street in downtown Toronto; he is blindfolded and has signs that read "I am a Muslim. I am labelled as a terrorist. I trust you. Do you trust me? Give me a hug." Needless to say, the video involved lots of people coming up to the chap and hugging him.

That assembly led to possibly the most satisfying week of my career in education so far: as I walked around the school, I witnessed lots of spontaneous hugging between students. I can't claim to have transformed their empathy levels in just 30 minutes, but what I had done was make them think about their own behaviour and what it means to demonstrate care for others. In every school, we should be asking young people to reflect on decency and what it means to be a good person.

I may be utterly biased, but I fully support those who say teaching is the noblest of professions. This chapter is a reminder that what we do in our classrooms goes far beyond preparing students for exams or assessments. We try and try again to help young people develop the qualities they will need when they enter the "real" world. What better or more important endeavour is there than to help children grow into empathetic and compassionate adults?

A quiet reflection

Miranda McKearney (@MirandaMcK) is the founder of the community interest organisation EmpathyLab, which uses high-quality literature to build children's empathy, literacy and social activism.

Young people are growing up in a society with a major empathy deficit; hate crimes are at their highest level since records began and there are growing concerns about the negative effects of social media. EmpathyLab sees empathy as a beacon of hope in our divided world; a much-needed force for connection and understanding – increased empathy is good for society and vital for young people's life chances. Psychologists highlight its central place in the bank of social and emotional skills young people need – without strong empathy skills, they will struggle to form the strong relationships they need to learn and thrive.

EmpathyLab aims to build children's empathy, literacy and social activism through a more systematic use of literature. Its strategy builds on scientific evidence showing the power of reading to build real-life empathy skills, and the organisation helps schools, libraries and authors integrate a sharper empathy focus into their work.

This short case study is from one of the 11 pioneer schools which EmpathyLab has worked with for three years.

Claire Williams, deputy head, Kenilworth Primary School, Hertfordshire:

"During 2016, we were shocked by series of incidents in which our children seemed absolutely incapable of realising that their actions had hurt others. We felt that empathy was disappearing from their lives and that it was essential to rebuild it. We got in touch with EmpathyLab.

After joining the pioneer group and attending training, we returned to school determined to put empathy at the heart of our development plan. It linked excellently to English and maths targets because you need empathy skills and emotional wellbeing to understand literature, access the curriculum and succeed in later life. We made our 2017/18 priorities maths, English and empathy.

We wanted the whole school community to use a common language surrounding empathy. We trained all staff and governors, making sure that we all meant the same thing and didn't confuse empathy with sympathy. We then introduced the topic to children through whole-school assemblies using different storybooks to support EmpathyLab's themes, including how to look from other people's perspectives, active listening and how body language gives you clues about people's real emotions. Within classes, each teacher adapted the excellent resources to further develop the understanding of empathy.

The children's enthusiasm led to us adopting the idea of playground 'empathy leaders', building on work done by Beck Primary [in Sheffield]. Children applied for these roles and are now available if other children need somebody to talk to. They wear their empathy leader jackets with pride. I had expected this role to need a lot of adult support – but I was incredibly wrong!

Engaging with EmpathyLab has had such a visible effect. When dealing with difficult situations, we now focus on the role of empathy. In turn the children now respond immediately to the idea of using their empathy skills, answering questions about the other person's point of view. They then use their empathy to find solutions, helping situations to be resolved constructively. They now view each other as supports, and have come a long way from the cohort that prioritised themselves and their own emotions.

The number of behaviour incidents has dropped significantly, from 147 in 2017 to 87. Exclusions have also reduced significantly. Our recent Ofsted inspection commended behaviour, stating: 'Leaders have based the curriculum plan on the importance of pupils' mental and physical well-being. This ... is also evident in the importance placed on being a good team member and the focus on empathy.'

The work has also had a significant effect on reading – children can identify how characters are feeling and explore these emotions at a far greater depth. For our reading SATs results, our progress measures rose by 1.8 points, and we are also seeing improvements in writing as the children create characters with greater depth. In Year 6, our writing progress score has risen 4.95 points."

Introspection

1. Is yours an empathy-rich classroom?

2. Do you engage in discussions about emotions and connecting with others?

3. Could your lesson content help to deepen compassion?

4. Do you celebrate moments in which empathy is demonstrated?

5. What other strategic plans could you make to develop empathy in your school?

A QUIET CONCLUSION

*Writing is a form of therapy; sometimes
I wonder how all those who do not write,
compose, or paint can manage to escape the
madness, melancholia, the panic and fear
which is inherent in a human situation*
Graham Greene

I will happily confess that writing this book was partly an act of therapy. I set off on a mission to unpick what it means to be quiet, unassuming and introverted in the extroverted world of schools – and I did so because that is entirely my own temperament.

I wanted to think about the many ways in which education could benefit from quiet virtues and skills. This was, in part, due to my frustration over the fact that quiet qualities are often overlooked – not just in education, but in the wider world. More needs to be done to keep quieter and more introverted teachers from feeling overwhelmed, from burning out, from being misunderstood by colleagues and from ultimately leaving the profession.

Being heard

This journey has given me hope. The voices of the many students and teachers who contributed to this book demonstrate just how powerfully present the advocates of quiet are in schools. Speaking to them has reminded me how richly complex we all are, and how vital it is to seek to genuinely understand and listen to others, especially those of different temperaments.

For children growing up in a divided and demanding world, this sensitivity and compassion is more necessary than ever. Schools should strive to be the most diverse and accepting of environments, helping to equip all young people with the self-confidence they need to thrive in education and beyond.

A quiet future

Teaching with empathy can help to lessen the stress and anxiety that the extrovert ideal can generate in the classroom. We must reflect on how much of what we ask quieter students to do requires them to alter or suppress their own natures. They should be helped to recognise, connect with and celebrate their strengths. They need to know that they are more than good enough, just as they are.

Without moments of introspection, I would argue that learning can never move beyond the superficial. Alongside the communication and dialogue that education requires, we need to create space for silence, individual reflection and deep thinking. As the poet Emily Dickinson once wrote, "Saying nothing sometimes says the most."

We also need to instil quiet and introspective skills in our students. These skills will help to prepare young people for the world beyond the school gates, and they have the potential to make their lives richer and better.

Embracing quieter values in the classroom could lead to improvements in teacher wellbeing and classroom practice, too. Consider just how loud a contemporary school can be and the restorative potential of quiet becomes clear. If we strip our teaching back to its essentials and set boundaries to preserve our work-life balance, we will be able to give our students our very best – and ensure that our careers in education are long ones.

Every teacher could benefit from the time and space to quietly engage with research, or to participate in meaningful discussion about what is taking place in their classroom. School management teams need to put energy into driving this forward: professional development with a quiet focus would help to prevent so much of the frustration that teachers currently feel over generic and repetitive CPD.

Be an idealist

Among the characteristics of more introverted individuals, apparently, are a deeply felt idealism, a sense of restlessness and a desire to create a better world. Some might argue that this book is naively idealistic; that it ignores the realities of modern life and clings to outdated values. Well, I'm fine with that.

If this idealistic book leads to just one student, who previously felt invisible, receiving a comment that recognises their hidden gifts, then it was worth writing. If it results in a teacher pausing before they utter "Jack is a delightful student, but is very quiet" at a parents' evening, and instead celebrating Jack's capacity to focus, listen and reflect, then I will be satisfied.

If one class is given the time and space to think deeply, then it has done its job. If one teacher, who might have been diligently striving to do their best but suffering from crippling self-doubt, begins to find confidence and a sense of purpose, then I will be happy.

Finally, if this book opens up a dialogue about the power of quiet virtues and their importance for young people – and their teachers – then our schools might just become richer, better and more empathetic places.

ACKNOWLEDGEMENTS

This book has been a hugely collaborative process and I could not have written it without the support of many friends, fellow teachers and family members.

I would like to thank my wife, Fiona, for her love, support and understanding at all times. Our introvert-extrovert dynamic is a brilliant combination. Fiona, I am very lucky that you bring out and encourage what is best in me.

Thank you to my mum and dad for their encouragement and excellent advice. They encapsulate all the quiet virtues. Any gems of pedagogical wisdom in this book – in Part I, in particular – are entirely down to my mum.

My thanks to all at John Catt, and in particular to Alex Sharratt for believing in the premise of the book. I am very grateful for the opportunity to write it. A huge thank you to the book's editor, Isla McMillan, who worked tirelessly to develop the manuscript. *A Quiet Education* is so much better for her careful attention to detail, sensitivity with language and immense clarity.

Thank you to all the wonderful educators who contributed their "quiet reflections". This book is so much richer and, I hope, so much more helpful for your insights. I am very grateful to those teachers, parents and young people who contacted me to share their thoughts on what education is like for quieter individuals. I hope the book does you justice.

Finally, a number of teachers read through my rambling early drafts and played a significant role in improving them. Thank you for being so generous with your time.

REFERENCES

Barton, C. (2018) *How I Wish I'd Taught Maths*. Woodbridge: John Catt Educational Ltd

Bazalgette, P. (2017) *The Empathy Instinct: How to Create a More Civil Society*. John Murray

Brian, D. (1996) *Einstein: A Life*. New York: John Wiley and Sons

Brown, PC, Roediger III, HL and McDaniel, MA. (2014) *Make It Stick: The Science of Successful Learning*. Cambridge, MA: Harvard University Press

Cain, S. (2013) *Quiet: The Power of Introverts in a World That Can't Stop Talking*. London: Penguin Books

Christodoulou, D. (2017) *Making Good Progress? The Future of Assessment for Learning*. Oxford: Oxford University Press

Csikszentmihalyi, M. (1996) *Creativity: The Work and Lives of 91 Eminent People*. HarperCollins

Csikszentmihalyi, M. (2002) *Flow: The Psychology of Happiness*. Rider

Curtis, C. (2015) "Girls Do Try and That Might Be Where the Problem Lies", *Learning From My Mistakes: An English Teacher's Blog*. Available at: tinyurl.com/smwc4aa (accessed 12 July 2019)

Dix, P. (2017) *When the Adults Change, Everything Changes: Seismic Shifts in School Behaviour*. Carmarthen: Independent Thinking Press

Education Endowment Foundation. (2018) *Metacognition and Self-Regulated Learning*. Available at: tinyurl.com/s5r74ye (accessed 12 September 2019)

Ellis, AK, Denton, DW and Bond, JB. (2014) "An Analysis of Research on Metacognitive Teaching Strategies", *Procedia: Social and Behavioral Sciences*, vol. 116

Ericsson, A. (2012) "The Danger of Delegating Education to Journalists", *Radical Eyes for Equity* (blog). Available at: tinyurl.com/rm8mcxr (accessed 10 August 2019)

Ericsson, A and Pool, R. (2016) *Peak: Secrets from the New Science of Expertise*. Vintage Digital

Firth, J. (2018) How to Learn: *Effective Study and Revision Methods for Any Course*. Arboretum Books

Flavell, JH. (1976) "Metacognitive Aspects of Problem Solving", in Resnick, LB (ed.) *The Nature of Intelligence* (pp. 231–236). Hillsdale, NJ: Lawrence Erlbaum

Goleman, D. (1996) Emotional Intelligence: *Why It Can Matter More Than IQ*. London: Bloomsbury Publishing

Goleman, D. (2013) *Focus: The Hidden Driver of Excellence*. London: Bloomsbury Publishing

Goleman, D and Davidson, RJ. (2017) *The Science of Meditation: How to Change Your Brain, Mind and Body*. London: Penguin Life

Grimmett, D. (2018) "Will You Be Quiet and Let Me Think?", *TL Ideas Blog*. Available at: tinyurl.com/r4v7v5d (accessed 15 March 2019)

Gross, R. (2015) *Psychology: The Science of Mind and Behaviour*. Hodder Education

Hansen, JR. (2005) *First Man: The Life of Neil A Armstrong*. Simon & Schuster

Helgoe, L. (2013) *Introvert Power: Why Your Inner Life is Your Hidden Strength*. Sourcebooks

Hendrick, C. and Macpherson, R. (2017) *What Does This Look Like in the Classroom? Bridging the Gap Between Research and Practice*. Woodbridge: John Catt Educational Ltd

Hochman, JC. and Wexler, N. (2017) *The Writing Revolution: A Guide to Advancing Thinking Through Writing in All Subjects and Grades*. Jossey-Bass

Jager, C. (2013) "Bill Gates: How to Succeed as an Introvert", *Lifehacker*. Available at: tinyurl.com/tutvuna (accessed 20 January 2019)

James, W. (1983) *Talks to Teachers on Psychology and to Students on Some of Life's Ideals*. Harvard University Press

Jung, CG. (1954) *The Development of Personality*. London: Routledge

Kahnweiler, JB. (2018) *The Introverted Leader: Building on Your Quiet Strength*. Berrett-Koehler Publishers

Konnikova, M. (2013) "Why Your Name Matters", *The New Yorker*. Available at: tinyurl.com/yx2ruavh (accessed 11 November 2018)

Lahey, J. (2013) "Introverted Kids Need to Learn to Speak Up at School", *The Atlantic*. Available at: tinyurl.com/tjrzxqv (accessed 31 January 2019)

Laney, MO. (2002) *The Introvert Advantage: How Quiet People Can Thrive in an Extrovert World*. Workman Publishing Company

Lees, H. (2012) *Silence in Schools*. Trentham Books

Lemov, D. (2010) *Teach Like a Champion: 49 Techniques That Put Students on the Path to College*. San Francisco, CA: Jossey-Bass

Lemov, D. (2015) *Teach Like a Champion 2.0: 62 Techniques That Put Students on the Path to College*. San Francisco, CA: Jossey-Bass

Levitin, DJ. (2015) *The Organized Mind: Thinking Straight in the Age of Information Overload.* London: Penguin Books

Little, BR. (2012) *Me, Myself and Us: The Science of Personality and the Art of Well-being.* PublicAffairs

Maitland, S. (2014) *How to Be Alone.* Macmillan

Mar, RA, Oatley, K and Peterson, JB. (2009) *Exploring the Link Between Reading Fiction and Empathy: Ruling Out Individual Differences and Examining Outcomes.* Available at: tinyurl.com/wqgbglk

Maraniss, D. (2013) *Barack Obama: The Story.* Simon & Schuster

Markway, BG and Markway, GP. (2003) *Painfully Shy: How to Overcome Social Anxiety and Reclaim Your Life.* St. Martin's Press

Naylor, P. (2018) "Physics Exam on Wednesday? We'll Be OK, We're Self-Regulating, Sir!", Blackpool Research School (blog). Available at: tinyurl.com/w7nr98c (accessed 15 September 2019)

Old, A. (2019) "Noise", *Scenes From the Battleground: Teaching in British Schools* (blog). Available at: tinyurl.com/trtusdq (accessed 15 March 2019)

Ollin, R. (2008) "Silent Pedagogy and Rethinking Classroom Practice: Structuring Teaching Through Silence Rather Than Talk", *Cambridge Journal of Education,* 38(2):265–280

Organisation for Economic Co-operation and Development. (2014) *TALIS 2013 Results: An International Perspective on Teaching and Learning.* OECD Publishing. Available at: tinyurl.com/ug4umgx (accessed 11 February 2019)

Pintrich, P. (2002) "The Role of Metacognitive Knowledge in Learning, Teaching, and Assessing", *Theory into Practice,* 41(4):219–225. Available at: tinyurl.com/yeb5wp9d

Pink, DH. (2010) *Drive: The Surprising Truth About What Motivates Us.* Canongate Books

Pinker, S. (2015) *The Sense of Style: The Thinking Person's Guide to Writing in the 21st Century.* Penguin

Pinkett, M. (2017) "Militant Tenderness: Modelling Positive Behaviours in Boys", *All Ears* (blog). Available at: tinyurl.com/ws2duzr (accessed 17 August 2019)

Pinkett, M and Roberts, M. (2019) *Boys Don't Try? Rethinking Masculinity in Schools.* Routledge

Rowe, MB. (1987) "Wait Time: Slowing Down May Be a Way of Speeding Up". *American Educator 11,* pp. 38–43

Sacks, O. (2015) *Gratitude.* Picador

Schultz, K. (2010) *Rethinking Classroom Participation: Listening to Silent Voices.* Teachers College Press

Severs, A. (2017) "The More-ness of Reading", *Reading Rocks* (blog). Available at: tinyurl.com/vg853ql

Shakespeare's Sister. (2014) "Because It Is My Name!", *Daily Kos.* Available at: tinyurl.com/qo36zkl (accessed 12 November 2019)

Sherrington, T. (2017) *The Learning Rainforest: Great Teaching in Real Classrooms.* Woodbridge: John Catt Educational Ltd

Sims, S and Fletcher-Wood, H. (2018) "Characteristics of Effective Teacher Professional Development: What We Know, What We Don't Know, How We Can Find Out", *Improving Teaching* (blog). Available at: tinyurl.com/w8gwhve (accessed 12 November 2019)

Smith, M and Firth, J. (2018) *Psychology in the Classroom: A Teacher's Guide to What Works.* Routledge

Soderstrom, NC and Bjork, RA. (2015) "Learning Versus Performance: An Integrative Review", *Perspectives on Psychological Science*, 10(2):176–199

Spencer, J. "Encouraging Introverts to Speak Up in School", *Quiet Revolution* (blog). Available at: tinyurl.com/v2uaco9 (accessed 14 March 2019)

Stoneman, C. (2019) "School Leadership: Dispositions and Knowledge", *Birmingham Teacher* (blog). Available at: tinyurl.com/yx64yvlm (accessed 12 May 2019)

Sweller, J. (1988) "Cognitive Load During Problem Solving: Effects on Learning", *Cognitive Science*, vol. 12, issue 2, pp. 257–285

Timperley, HS, Parr, JM and Bertanees, C. (2009) "Promoting Professional Inquiry for Improved Outcomes for Students in New Zealand", *Professional Development in Education*, v35, n2, pp. 227–245

Vygotsky, LS. (1962) *Thought and Language.* Cambridge, MA: MIT Press

Whitehouse, C. (2011) *Effective Continuing Professional Development for Teachers.* Centre for Education Research and Policy. Available at: tinyurl.com/tkjg5zb (accessed 12 November 2019)

Whyte, WH. (1956) *The Organization Man.* Simon & Schuster

Willingham, DT. (2010) *Why Don't Students Like School? A Cognitive Scientist Answers Questions About How the Mind Works and What It Means for the Classroom.* London: Jossey-Bass